ASPERGER'S SYNDROME AND MINDFULNESS

of related interest

Asperger Syndrome and Anxiety
A Guide to Successful Stress Management
Nick Dubin
ISBN 978 1 84310 895 5

Mind/Body Techniques for Asperger's Syndrome
The Way of the Pathfinder
Ron Rubio
Paperback ISBN 978 1 84310 875 7

The Complete Guide to Asperger's Syndrome
Tony Attwood
Hardback ISBN 978 1 84310 495 7
Paperback ISBN 978 1 84310 669 2

A Self-Determined Future with Asperger Syndrome
Solution Focused Approaches
E. Veronica Bliss and Genevieve Edmonds
ISBN 978 1 84310 513 8

ASPERGER'S SYNDROME AND MINDFULNESS

Taking Refuge in the Buddha

CHRIS MITCHELL

Jessica Kingsley *Publishers*
London and Philadelphia

First published in 2009
by Jessica Kingsley Publishers
116 Pentonville Road
London N1 9JB, UK
and
400 Market Street, Suite 400
Philadelphia, PA 19106, USA

www.jkp.com

Library of Congress Cataloging in Publication Data
Mitchell, Chris, 1978-
  Asperger's syndrome and mindfulness : taking refuge in the Buddha / Chris Mitchell.
    p. cm.
  ISBN 978-1-84310-686-9 (pb : alk. paper)
  1. Asperger's syndrome. 2. Memory. 3. Attention. 4. Buddhist meditations. 5.
Meditation--Buddhism. 6. Theravada Buddhism--Doctrines. I. Title.
  RC553.A88M58 2008
  616.85'8832--dc22
                        2008019689
British Library Cataloguing in Publication Data
A CIP catalogue record for this book is available from the British Library

ISBN 978 1 84310 686 9

Printed and bound in the United States

Nammo Tassa Bhagavato Arahato
Sammā Sambuddhassa

'Honour to the blessed one,
perfectly and completely
awakened one'

In memory of

Genevieve Edmonds 1981–2008

On returning home from a trip to India and Nepal, including visits to Buddhist pilgrimage sites, during February 2008, I came home to some very sad news when I was informed of the tragic death of Genevieve Edmonds, who initially encouraged me to write this book as well as inviting me to contribute to her publications *Asperger's Syndrome and Employment* and *Asperger's Syndrome and Social Relationships*, also published by Jessica Kingsley Publishers. As well as having much respect for Genevieve as a role model and an advocate for Asperger's Syndrome, she had also become a very good friend.

Genevieve had some wonderful qualities, very kind, understanding and selflessness, qualities emphasised strongly within Buddhism. The Asperger community has lost someone very special, who made a real difference in terms of understanding Asperger's Syndrome in a positive way through her work with the ASPECT group at the University of Sheffield Hallam and disability consultancy service Paradigm.

Rest in peace Genevieve, free from dukkhā, for what you have left behind in terms of your work will help to alleviate much of the dukkhā that is living for many people diagnosed with Asperger's Syndrome.

Contents

Acknowledgements

There are many people in my life who mean a lot to me. Unfortunately there isn't quite enough room to name all, but those I send much compassion to include:

My family, including my parents, grandparents, siblings, aunts, uncles and cousins for all your continued support.

All individuals with Asperger's Syndrome and their families and carers whom I provided support to. Working with you and knowing you has raised my own self-esteem giving me so much joy to see that I have made a difference to your lives in a positive way.

Lynne Moxon, Chartered Psychologist, for all your help over the years since my diagnosis.

Christine Haugh, University of Middlesex, for all your encouragement.

Professor Tony Attwood, whose work initially helped me realise who I am as a person diagnosed with Asperger's Syndrome.

Clare Sainsbury, author of *Martian in the Playground*, for introducing me to the Asperger community through Autuniv-1 all those years ago.

Garry Burge and his family, the first friend diagnosed with Asperger's Syndrome I got to know well.

Tara Kimberley Torme, the first female diagnosed with Asperger's Syndrome I got to know well.

Dr Dawn Prince-Hughes, editor of *Aquamarine Blue 5: Personal Stories of College Students with Autism,* for all your advice and support over the years.

The members of the NAS Asperger Social Group in Sunderland, for reassuring me that I am not alone.

Peter Harvey, Professor of Buddhist Studies, University of Sunderland, for all your help and guidance with meditation practice, helping me realise the benefits of bringing the qualities achieved during meditation practice into everyday life.

Venerable Ajahn Nandapala, Research Student in Buddhist Studies and Theravāda Buddhist Monk in the Burmese Tradition, for your guidance and insight on the teachings of the Buddha.

Ajahn Munindo and the monastic community at Aruna Ratanagiri, Harnham, Northumberland, for your guidance.

I would also like to take this opportunity to extend my compassion to all my former school teachers (primary and secondary), college/university lecturers and colleagues past, present and future, realising how difficult understanding must have been on your part.

The author in Sarnath, India. The stupa in the background is where the Buddha is said to have given his first teachings 2500 years ago.

Note on Terminology and Pronunciation

Where possible, the author of this work has looked to avoid jargon, particularly in relation to Pāli, the written language of the Buddhist scriptures (the Pāli Canon). Only where it was felt necessary were Pāli terms used, particularly when describing meditation practice. Pāli terms used within this work, with their phonetic pronunciation and meaning, are detailed below:

- **Dhamma** (*dham-ma*) – This word has several levels of meaning, including:

  ○ the way things are in and of themselves

  ○ the Buddha's teachings about the way things are

  ○ the practice of the Buddha's teachings in training the mind.

- **Dhammapāda** (*dham-ma-par-dah*) – 'Path of the Dhamma', one of the most important scriptures contained in the Pāli Canon.

- **Dukkhā** (*du-kha*) – Suffering, hardship, uneasiness.

- **Khandha** (*kan-dah*) – A component part of sensory perception including:

  ○ **Rūpa** (*roo-pa*) – physical phenomena

  ○ **Vedanā** (*ved-an-ar*) – feelings of pleasure, pain or indifference

  ○ **Saññā** (*san-nnyy-ar*) – concepts, labels, allusions

- ○ **Saṅkhāra** (*sa-ny-kar-ra*) – mental fashioning, formations
- ○ **Viññāṇa** (*vi-nnyy-ar-nah*) – sensory consciousness.
- **Mettā** (*met-tar*) – Loving-kindness, compassion.
- **Papañca** (*pa-pa-ny-chah*) – Proliferation.
- **Samatha** (*sam-at-ha*) – Calm.
- **Theravāda** (*t-hera-var-da*) – 'Way of the elders', the tradition of Buddhism discussed in this work.
- **Vipassanā** (*vi-pass-an-ar*) – Insight.

Pronunciation guide

- A bar over a vowel makes it long, e.g. *ā* is pronounced 'ar', like in **bar**n.
- Aspirated consonants are accompanied by a strong breath pulse from the chest, e.g. *th* is pronounced 't-h', like in hot-**h**ouse.
- When aspirated consonants occur as part of a cluster, the aspiration comes at the end of the cluster, e.g.
  - ○ *c* is pronounced 'ch', like in **ch**art
  - ○ *ñ* is pronounced 'ny', like in ca**ny**on
  - ○ *ññ* is pronounced 'nnyy'.
- Double consonants are pronounced long, e.g. *ss* is like 'ss' in unnece**ss**ary.
- When there is an accent under the letter (e.g. **ṇ**), it indicates a cerebral letter. It is pronounced with the tongue touching the upper bridge of the mouth.
- *ṅ* is an 'ng', nasal sound said from the mouth rather than the nose.

Many thanks to Peter Harvey, Professor of Buddhist Studies, University of Sunderland, for his assistance in preparing this pronunciation guide.

CHAPTER 1

Introduction

The path of Asperger's Syndrome

Being diagnosed with Asperger's Syndrome back in 1998, when I was 20 years old, was an immediate relief. Having had my diagnosis for almost ten years at the time of writing, I have found that beyond the impermanent nature of relief, Asperger's Syndrome is a lifelong journey, following a path. At times, this path can be difficult to negotiate, but with the right effort and through developing self-esteem, the path of Asperger's Syndrome can also be a fulfilling one to follow through life, if one is able to 'awaken' to it through development of awareness.

Mindfulness is a technique, or state of mind, where one becomes intentionally aware of their way of thoughts, including being aware of how different thoughts arise, which provides for open, non-judgemental thought. This technique, if one makes the effort to cultivate and develop it through practice described throughout this work, is helpful for a person with Asperger's Syndrome, in terms of being able to effectively assess oneself in relation to one's surroundings, and is just as helpful for a person not on the autistic spectrum, in terms of understanding Asperger's Syndrome in a judgement-free way.

As described in the Dhammapāda (a major Buddhist scripture), the mind is fickle and flighty, swaying between thought, almost like a hyperactive child. As a person with Asperger's

Syndrome, I find that the way the mind can behave in terms of expressing so many different thoughts at once can lead to much stress, which is why it helps me to concentrate the mind through meditation. The Buddha developed meditation as a way to cultivate the mind from yoga techniques that existed in India over 2500 years ago. Meditation is not unique to Buddhism, as other major beliefs involve forms of meditation, and one doesn't have to be religious or spiritual to meditate, as it can be an effective therapy for good health regarding the immune and breathing systems as well as for relaxation. For me, as a person with Asperger's Syndrome, meditation is a useful therapy for anxiety and low self-esteem as well as a tool for relaxation.

Though I experienced much personal joy at the moment of diagnosis, I was also faced with many questions about myself. The direction in which my life was heading was about to change. For the first time in my life, after being diagnosed I was able to make an effective assessment of myself in terms of my strengths and weaknesses, so that I could adapt myself as a person with Asperger's Syndrome to an appropriate lifestyle. This was initially hard for me, especially after coming out of university where I couldn't find much, if any, appropriate support or guidance, largely due to general lack of awareness of Asperger's Syndrome, among the services I sought.

What I needed to find was the right path, one that I could manage. At first, I had hoped that all the problems that I had experienced in my life would 'disappear' once diagnosed and that the journey through life would be easier. In many ways I was wrong. In one way or another, all of us – people with Asperger's Syndrome, people with related conditions such as ADHD (attention deficit hyperactivity disorder) or high-functioning autism and those who are not on the autistic spectrum – experience life's 'ups and downs'. Rather than 'eliminating' them or simply pretending that they don't exist, it is often a question of managing them effectively so that one is not so hindered by them. Until I began to explore the teachings of the

Buddha in more detail, I didn't realise that this was something that I could manage on my own as a person with Asperger's Syndrome.

Like Asperger's Syndrome, Buddhism involves following a path – the Eightfold Path – which incorporates the Four Noble Truths in the Buddha's teachings. These are:

1. suffering
2. origin of suffering
3. cessation of suffering
4. the Eightfold Path, or the Middle Way.

Relating to what I have experienced as a person with Asperger's Syndrome, both undiagnosed and diagnosed, I have found the Four Noble Truths conducive towards understanding my own suffering as well as how to recognise it and manage it, so that I am not as affected by it.

The First Noble Truth, that of suffering, helps me to understand that living is suffering, not just for myself, but for others too, both those diagnosed with Asperger's Syndrome and those not on the autistic spectrum. How one perceives and experiences suffering varies dramatically. As a person with Asperger's Syndrome, much personal unhappiness I have experienced relates to general non-satisfaction with life in terms of disappointments I have experienced or what I feel that I have missed out on in life. Many adults with Asperger's Syndrome I have met appear to share the view that there are things missing from their life, often related to social isolation.

Recognising the sources of suffering lies in the Second Noble Truth, that of origin of suffering. People with Asperger's Syndrome often have obsessive-compulsive tendencies and can develop narrow fixations, leading to difficulty with flexible thinking. This can lead to one of the main causes of suffering that the Buddha taught, that of attachment. Readers of autism literature will know about how some people diagnosed with

Asperger's Syndrome can develop obsessive interests, including building up extensive collections. Though having such interests isn't un-normal, it can lead to suffering for a person with Asperger's Syndrome as it can distance them from others socially, leading to isolation. Another cause of suffering the Buddha identified is that of craving, wanting things. Many people with Asperger's Syndrome are no different to others in terms of wanting things, but it may be more difficult to notice why they may experience suffering, courtesy of this, in terms of how they may experience anxiety wanting something. This, in turn, leads to the Third Noble Truth, that of cessation of suffering.

If a person with Asperger's Syndrome is able to develop an intuitive awareness of their causes of suffering, they can realise the truth about who they are. This can be a long and, at times, mentally arduous journey. Many people diagnosed with Asperger's Syndrome have had to travel further than most to find out who they really are, in terms of finding a diagnosis and being able to adapt to it and appreciate it, before finding that there are others diagnosed with the condition who may share similar experiences in terms of suffering. The insight this provides can also help with cessation of suffering.

The route to cessation of suffering follows in the Fourth Noble Truth, the Eightfold Path or 'the Middle Way'. What is so often confusing for a person with Asperger's Syndrome is not being able to grasp unwritten rules or guidance, including those in relation to social situations and managing life generally. For me, following the Middle Way has not only helped me under-stand and cope with my own suffering, but I find it also helps me recognise my place in the world around me so much better, including how I relate to others. The Middle Way comprises:

1. Right Understanding

2. Right-directed Thought

3. Right Speech

4. Right Action

5. Right Livelihood

6. Right Effort

7. Right Mindfulness

8. Right Concentration.

The first point of the Middle Way is that of Right Understanding: helping one to develop a non-judgemental approach towards the world around them by awakening to understanding how biases can distance one from truth. To enable this, the second point is that of Right-directed Thought, that is thought arising out of neutrality.

How a person diagnosed with Asperger's Syndrome interprets speech is often variable, depending on the individual. Some may interpret metaphors and other figures of speech more literally than others. I have found that I, and some other people with the condition I know, can be mentally hurt by attempted cynical humour. The third point of the Middle Way, that of Right Speech, is a helpful guideline in terms of avoiding harsh or malicious speech, and to avoid back-biting if one feels they have been spoken to incorrectly. The next two points, Right Action and Right Livelihood, are more moral guidelines for living, including not taking what is not given and not engaging in wrong physical behaviour, including resorting to violence.

The remaining three points are qualities that can be developed from meditation practice: Right Effort, Right Mindfulness and Right Concentration. Gaining a balance between Right Mindfulness and Right Concentration applied with Right Effort can enable a person with Asperger's Syndrome to retain the strengths that their condition provides, such as ability to specialise through concentration, while remaining close to truth through mindfulness – a quality much referred to in this book.

I have begun to realise some of these qualities of the mind through practice of meditation, as taught in the Theravāda tradition as practised in Thailand. This book isn't intended as instruction or guidance on how to practise meditation. Probably the best way to learn and practise meditation is through attending a class taught by an experienced meditator. As I refer to meditation experiences throughout this book, it will help for me to briefly explain some aspects of my practice. A fundamental technique for sustaining attention is focusing awareness on the body; traditionally, this is practised while sitting or walking. The two main stages of meditation that I practise are:

- **Samatha** – Meaning 'calm' in Pāli, Samatha focuses on the breath, helping to calm the mind, concentrating mental energy, enabling one to experience feelings of peace and calmness, enabling clarity of thought. Samatha practice involves recognising different stages of breathing, starting from one's longest comfortable breath to shorter breaths and other stages of breathing, some of which involve counting. When applied effectively, through being able to focus on the breath, Samatha can enable one to concentrate their mental energy, rather like steadying a shaking bowl of water.

- **Vipassanā** – Meaning 'insight' in Pāli, Vipassanā is used to achieve insight into the true nature of things, which is much more difficult than one may think. Often we tend to interpret and see our surroundings based on our preconceptions, opinions, past experiences and other related issues. The clarity of thought enabled through Samatha practice enables one to recollect their thoughts and be able to reflect on past, present and potential future experiences. This enables one to see the true nature of the way we are and the way things are.

In addition, I have also learned techniques of loving-kindness meditation to help extend my sympathies and benevolence as far afield as possible, even as far as hostile people, including bullies. This helps me avoid attaching accusations of blame to people from both my past and present.

I had been wanting to try such an activity because I had been experiencing much anxiety and wanted to find an effective way or therapy to help me cope with it. While I have been practising I have found it very beneficial to my daily life, in terms of how it helps me cope with issues I experience related to being diagnosed with Asperger's Syndrome, including anxiety and frustration.

Though I practise meditation, I don't consider myself a 'Buddhist' as such, as this would attach me to it, to the point where it could become an Asperger's Syndrome-like fixation. My reason for deciding to follow the Middle Way was to relieve myself from such excessive attachment, which has so often isolated me as a person with Asperger's Syndrome in the past. When asked about my belief, I prefer to describe myself as being 'one who takes refuge in the Buddha'. Like other faiths, Buddhism has different schools. I follow the Theravāda tradition as it is more of an individual pursuit, which I have found adaptable to my needs.

Not all people diagnosed with Asperger's Syndrome may find Buddhism suitable in a similar way, especially since the many people with the condition come from different faith backgrounds and have different individual needs. For me though, I find Buddhism conducive to my needs as a person with Asperger's Syndrome as it enables me to see the truth about who I am in terms of my condition, rather than suffer by hiding it or pretending to be normal.

The stronger awareness I feel I have developed through meditation has also enabled me to realise more closely that it is not only a person with Asperger's Syndrome that can experience the confusion and frustration associated with it. As well as affecting the individual with the condition, it can also affect their surroundings, including their immediate family. People from my past whom I have since caught up with feel they missed out on knowing me for whom I am, and in some cases even experienced their own frustration feeling they could not get through to me. Sadly, this can lead to ill-will – one of the Five Hindrances identified in the Buddha's teachings.

Since first being asked to give talks and workshops about Asperger's Syndrome, I have felt it a duty to work towards increasing understanding of the condition, so that others diagnosed with it can avoid the very worst experiences of those like myself and some of my closest friends diagnosed with Asperger's Syndrome late in life. In this book I will start from the Five Hindrances and how they can affect a person with Asperger's Syndrome directly and indirectly, before looking at different situations and including suggestions for how both people with Asperger's Syndrome and those not on the autistic spectrum can understand one another better, before eventually looking at overcoming the hindrances through recognising the Five Spiritual Faculties.

Though the Middle Way can provide good guidance for living to those who choose to follow it, it is up to the individual to develop the qualities, enabling one to both appreciate and recognise living more clearly, leading to happiness and eventual enlightenment: 'The Awakened Ones can but point the way, we must make the effort ourselves' (The Dhammapada, Verse 276, as translated by Munindo 2006).

CHAPTER 2

Asperger's Syndrome and the Five Hindrances

The Buddha's teachings suggest that there are five hindrances in our lives – a hindrance refers to a negative state of mind or an unmindful state. The opposite of mindfulness, an unmindful state is where one is unintentionally aware of their thought in relation to their surroundings. For instance, when frustrated, one may not be aware of the source of the frustration, and at the other extreme, when excited, one may not be aware of their immediate vulnerabilities. Many people with Asperger's Syndrome, including myself, often experience 'mental block-ages' in relation to frustration and anxiety, which often make such issues difficult to cope with, thus 'hindering' one's ability to cope effectively. The Five Hindrances are:

1. sense desire

2. ill-will

3. sloth and torpor

4. restlessness and remorse

5. doubt.

These hindrances are with almost everyone in day-to-day life in various shapes and forms. For me, and for many others with Asperger's Syndrome, they represent issues that we often experience much difficulty in being able to cope with. To give an idea of how the Five Hindrances affect me, I will use five examples from my own life.

Sense desire

For me, this hindrance often arises out of personal frustration through things being the way they are, in terms of thinking that 'as a person with Asperger's Syndrome, for what I have experienced in my life, I deserve to have it better'. In thinking along the lines of 'having it better', one may find oneself giving unwise attention to beautiful, often material, images and items, building up an image of 'how I should have it'.

Like most, I do sometimes find myself being drawn towards beautiful and material items, from cars to attractive members of the opposite sex. In most societies it is difficult not to be, considering the number of adverts/commercials that one sees in day-to-day life on television, billboards, etc. Want of different material items for a person with Asperger's Syndrome can come from different sources, depending on the perception of the individual. It could arise from an interest or obsession that leads to a collection (e.g. toy cars, model trains). Much Buddhist literature compares sense desire to 'being in debt'. Though it is possible that a person with Asperger's Syndrome may run into debt by acquiring items they collect and hoard in an obsessive way, personally I have often experienced fear of running up debt through excessive purchase of desirable items.

Where I have experienced difficulty with sense desire as a person with Asperger's Syndrome has been in social situations, where people around me are engaged in conversations about personal success, which is often material based. While I feel insular, like a seed frozen in time, people around me are moving on with their lives both professionally, through being promoted at work and earning high salaries, and socially, making high-profile contacts through networking, developing relationships before getting married and starting families and getting onto the property ladder. Such transitions among people around my age are common topics of conversation to which I can't relate, resulting in social isolation and low self-esteem.

Ill-will

Having Asperger's Syndrome, I am often seen as having a rather complex personality. I find that others don't understand that emotional issues affect me very differently. On my part, I don't often understand how differently such issues affect others. This can cause misunderstandings on both sides, leading to teething troubles in social relationships. By 'teething troubles', I mean how I may misunderstand how someone new I meet says something to me or, alternatively, not know how to respond to someone new I meet, not being able to anticipate how they may interpret it.

This is why I can still, at times, unintentionally hurt or upset someone through something I say. If I don't know or haven't been introduced to another person, it can be easy for me, when just trying to be friendly, to make a comment that turns out to be unintentionally upsetting or offensive to another person. As well as hurting the person that it upsets or offends, it can also hurt me in the sense that I can understand how the person I have unintentionally upset or offended is feeling, being vulnerable to such misunderstandings myself. It can hurt me emotionally if I feel I have hurt someone, in the sense that I can feel guilty, which in turn leads to worry.

From such teething troubles, it is easy to develop feelings of ill-will towards someone. Where I have developed ill-feelings towards others is often through not just what they say to me, but in what context they say it. For instance, I can sometimes get hurt when a person uses humour towards me in a cynical way. I understand that certain people may be comfortable with or find fun in cynical or acerbic humour directed at a colleague, be it for fun or to assert superiority. For me though, regardless of the intention, to be on the receiving end of this type of humour can sometimes be hurtful in the sense that I can feel someone is trying to make me feel inadequate or trying to belittle me.

When one feels they have been misunderstood by so many, as I feel I often have been through my life and can still be, it is very easy to feel discriminated against. What it helps me to remember though is that not everybody I meet is going to know why I am the way I am, and that everybody has assumptions, and this can also work the opposite way in terms of how I treat others. Just because I may not be happy with the way someone has treated me, or someone feels as though I have treated them badly, doesn't mean that ill-will of any kind is intended. Sometimes though this can be very difficult for me, as a person with Asperger's Syndrome, to recognise.

Sloth and torpor

This hindrance, I feel, can emerge from lack of confidence, where one's mind can become almost dormant, turning into sludge or putty, through not being able to see a way out of it. The general difficulty with flexible thinking that a person with Asperger's Syndrome may experience can contribute to this hindrance. By flexible thinking, I mean the ability to consider thoughts, views and opinions different to their own way of thinking, including being able to view events and situations from different perspectives.

Where a person with Asperger's Syndrome can experience this hindrance is within situations that involve negotiation and debate, such as making a sale or in a seminar or meeting situation. If the person has much difficulty with flexible thought, it may be very difficult for them to find the mental energy to challenge different points of argument during debate or suggestions offered during negotiations.

It can often be more apparent when a person with Asperger's Syndrome has an argument they want to put across, often with extensively researched information to support it, and they find themselves unable to respond when challenged. It was often very difficult for me during seminars at university to be able to find the energy to collect my thoughts and put across an appropriate response whenever a point I made had been challenged.

Restlessness and remorse

Of the Five Hindrances, the fourth is the one that perhaps affects me most of all in relation to my Asperger's Syndrome, in the sense that there are many personal issues that I am unsure of or worry about. Many of these worries relate to uncertainty faced in situations where I can't predict or anticipate. Such situations are often related to my living and working arrangements. Regarding my working arrangements, uncertainty that I occasionally feel includes how much longer I will be doing my current job before moving on, and if and when I move on what will I be doing and how much change will there be in terms of tasks, duties, responsibilities and location? Similarly, if for any reason I was to move to a home in a different town, it would be difficult for me to anticipate how my life would be in relation to a new environment, including how long it would take for me to feel settled. I have experienced depression in relation to such uncertainty. In this sense, depression is a high-level form of this hindrance.

The fourth hindrance so often affects me when doing something beyond the comfort zone of my routine, such as doing something different or unusual at a particular time of a day or week. This could involve having to travel at relatively short notice (e.g. an emergency meeting) to somewhere I am not used to going, where I have to find my way by car or public transport and, when attempting to make my way there, I can experience anxiety.

Doubt

Where this hindrance affects me as a person with Asperger's Syndrome is when I have to complete something, which could be an academic course, a training programme or a journey, or when setting personal goals and targets. For example, I considered quitting university midway through my degree. This was largely induced by anxiety relating to whether or not it would be worth completing the degree in terms of how useful it would be.

From childhood, I have often been a slow learner, often taking a little longer than most to learn new skills and tasks to the appropriate standard. This can lead to others thinking that I am either not good enough or to make assumptions that I will never achieve what I set out to. Having faced such negativity in the past, I have found that it can be easy to start doubting oneself before starting on such a journey. Such playbacks are so often played by the tape-recorder that is the mind, so that one becomes attached to them.

Where else this hindrance affects me is when I experience difficulty in relation to starting something new, such as a new job – I can find myself doubting my suitability for the job. Even if I have been doing a job for a while, and experience difficulty, I can find myself doubting my ability to do the job any more.

When setting goals and targets, I often assess problems that I may encounter along the way, but sometimes this can also nourish doubt in the sense that I begin to question whether I would be able to handle such difficulties if and when they arose. This can lead to me thinking that I have already failed before even attempting.

Often, we only notice the hindrances when related issues affect us. For example, when going through periods of depression and low self-esteem it may be due to doubt, in the sense that one is uncertain of their future, or restlessness and remorse, in that one may be troubled by present issues. What I have found helpful though is that recognising their existence where possible can help a person with Asperger's Syndrome overcome any issues they may experience in relation to the hindrances. Having an understanding of what hindrances are and what form they could potentially take, opens one up to awareness of the potential effects a particular hindrance may have. For example, when experiencing a period of anxiety, stress or depression, one can begin to think about and reflect on such feelings in the context of the hindrances. As I often experience much difficulty in being able to think logically in terms of taking appropriate action whenever the above or similar issues associated with the Five Hindrances affect me, being aware of their existence in various shapes or forms at least helps me anticipate related issues and events so that where possible I can avoid panicking.

When such issues are affecting me, I find that my mind can become full of negative and sometimes apathetic thought. Such thought clouds my mind to the extent that I can lose both mindfulness and concentration, so that I can only see how the issue is affecting myself in the context of the present, not focus on how it relates to others around me and my own future, both immediate and long-term, including long-term social relationships. This is why I have found that immediate or quick-fix solutions to problems very rarely work out.

Loss of mindfulness and concentration also makes it very difficult for me to realise the potential consequences that actions I may take could have for others. Why this particular aspect can be so sad for me is that I don't consider myself to be the sort of person who would purposely create ill-will among others and I don't like to make enemies. But if and when an action I take in any shape or form leads to ill-will or grudges between myself and others, I am often unsure of what has caused it, making it very difficult to rectify. For instance, in social situations, both formal (e.g. staff meetings) and informal (dinners, parties, etc.), it is difficult to understand the different unwritten rules or protocols between situations as they are often unexplained or unwritten.

In this book, I will cover themes that affect my day-to-day life as a person with Asperger's Syndrome who takes refuge in the Buddha, sometimes referring to the Five Hindrances, including where I feel practice has enabled me to overcome being conditioned by the hindrances and how it can help to be aware of the hindrances but not attached to them, before looking at how I am able, to an extent, to overcome them.

CHAPTER 3

Starting with Who You Are

How the easiest person to like can be you

Many people diagnosed with Asperger's Syndrome, including myself, often experience low self-esteem. In my case, I find that I experience very varying levels of self-esteem both low and high. Factors that contribute to low self-esteem vary greatly between different individuals with Asperger's Syndrome.

It can be very easy for a person with Asperger's Syndrome to experience low self-esteem through social isolation, particularly if the person genuinely would like to develop friendships and generally fit in socially but can't understand how to, while it appears to come quickly for others. Having experienced this myself, something I have found is how easy it is to not like or even hate oneself. This was especially true during my adolescent years when my contemporaries were developing relationships, both social and romantic.

Tibetan monks start with their mothers as the easiest person to like, especially since they brought them into the world. In Theravāda Buddhism though, the focus of who is the easiest person to like is oneself. Initially this may sound self-important or even egotistic, but the focus on liking oneself within the Theravāda tradition is more about finding the positive aspects and personal qualities one may have, that in some cases perhaps one wasn't previously aware of, before applying these qualities to how they relate to others. This includes being able to take one's frustrating experiences and curtail them in such a way that one can even see positive actions from where frustrations originate.

Frustrations that appear to be common in a lot of people with Asperger's Syndrome, including myself and other adults diagnosed with the condition that I have met, include:

- Inability to achieve as good grades/exam results at school/university as others, despite feeling they have had to put in much more effort.

- Not being able to find a job despite feeling they have so much to offer as a potential employee.

- Not being able to hold down a permanent job despite being a largely punctual and consistent employee.

- Inability to make friends easily despite considering themselves very loyal and generous.

- Inability to form an intimate relationship despite feeling they are a very caring, loyal individual while others appear to take their partners for granted.

I often ask myself questions about why issues such as those described above continue to affect me. This can make me dislike myself, thinking that I am not 'moving on' with my life, socially and professionally, like many of my former student colleagues and other contemporaries appear to be doing. It can be easy for me to think of myself as a failure because I have had so many problems with these and other issues.

Personally though, I feel that many individuals diagnosed with Asperger's Syndrome may be more skilled socially than they may think. Common myths and stereotypes often associated with Asperger's Syndrome suggest that people diagnosed with the condition have difficulty with empathy, that is they find it difficult to understand others' feelings and emotions. But many people with Asperger's Syndrome do experience deep emotional thought themselves, through issues such as frustration, and may actually understand better than most how others who experience such circumstances may feel. I have found that people with Asperger's Syndrome are more able than many may expect to think in depth about emotions, especially in relation to frustration and anxiety, and can develop a good understanding of these and related emotional issues. This is one of a number of reasons why I think many people with Asperger's Syndrome can be effective as learning mentors or support workers for people with learning disabilities, as well as possibly being good managers or trainers, as they may have a good understanding of the anxiety that a beginner learning a task may experience.

As a person with Asperger's Syndrome, I am primarily a visual thinker, in that I think in images and often focus on the detail within. Though this way of thinking can have its advantages in terms of self-esteem, as I often discuss when speaking publicly about my experiences of Asperger's Syndrome, visual thinking can also have problems. Such problems can emerge in a visual thinker when seeing images of success and prosperity around oneself in everyday life through different sources, including events that occur around me or what I see on television or in newspapers and magazines. As such images can become fixated in my mind once I see them, it is very difficult for me to 'delete' them. In this way, my mind can become like a digital camera without an erase facility.

The more such images build up in one's mind, the more they can eventually develop into a bigger image of what one may aspire to be or to achieve. I have experienced this often as have many other individuals with Asperger's Syndrome. Where I feel I have experienced this particularly was at university. When entering university, I wanted to make a new start, living in a different place, albeit still within reach of home, and meet new people – what one would imagine most young people want when going away to university and living away from home for the first time. I was initially eager to get away from home because I felt there were so many 'ghosts' around that represented some difficult times of my recent past. When I got to university though, and found that it didn't match the mental image that had built up in my mind, I quickly became disappointed and thus became unhappy. From this, and other similar experiences, I have learned that such mental images that build up in one's mind can easily stray from the truth, in terms of what may lie behind them.

To build up a mental image of what one aspires to be can often put pressure on oneself to the extent that one can experience high levels of disappointment in that one feels one can't live up to what one ideally would like to be. Like other people with Asperger's Syndrome, I have often thought of myself in relation to my contemporaries. For many people, the 'normal' trajectory of life appears to involve graduation, meeting partner, career development from entry level through to promotion, marriage, moving into first home together and eventually starting a family. Meanwhile, my life trajectory has been largely frozen in the sense that I have often struggled to hold down a steady career and have never unravelled the mystery of forming an intimate relationship. A close friend of mine, Garry Burge, who has Asperger's Syndrome, and who has experienced a life trajectory similar to my own, likened this experience to being like a 'seed frozen in time'.

Something that I have found when comparing myself to others whom I feel have it better than I do or have things that I would like to have, is that it is not good for my self-esteem, because it makes me want to be somebody I am not, leading to frustration. Even more so, comparing myself to others distances me from who I really am, almost to the point where I forget the positive aspects about myself, and how those positive aspects relate to people whom I am close to. When such thoughts enter my mind, I have found that it helps to identify their roots, rather than confront them directly. For instance, when a negative mental image is captured inside the digital camera which is my mind, rather than immediately press the erase button to rid it from my mind, I look to identify what is causing it, and then let it slowly evaporate, rather than reacting to it angrily, which may induce excessive anxiety. In this way, I find it best to let go of *what* I am and focus on *who* I am.

Without meaning to sound egotistic or 'up myself', personally, I like to think that my good qualities are that I am a very positive individual, I am able to treat others as individuals in relation to my own needs as an individual, I don't like to judge others by my own standards and where possible I like to encourage confidence in different people that I meet, especially if they have difficulty with self-esteem. As I have experienced unhappiness in relation to these particular themes, and to some extent even prejudice, I am able to understand how others who have experienced similar issues may feel. Such an understanding, I feel, enables me to be very tolerant and I am able to relate the good aspects of my personality to others, especially others diagnosed with Asperger's Syndrome I have become very close to. Also, the more that I have found myself able to relate the good aspects of my personality to others, the more I have come to realise the values of the good qualities in other people, including other people diagnosed with Asperger's Syndrome.

Since I started meditation, I have learned that the easiest person to like can be who you actually are if you focus on your good qualities, and this can be a route to self-confidence and, ultimately, personal happiness. It has enabled me to feel that who I am means much to those close to me, including my family, friends and people who feel my help has made a positive difference to their lives.

How to value who you are

For a person to value him- or herself is to like who they are. This might initially take some effort for a person with Asperger's Syndrome, particularly if they have suffered low self-esteem or depression, but some basic steps to take towards liking oneself include:

- Focus on positive aspects of yourself that you like, for example, you may feel you are caring and/or loyal.

- Try to identify where others like you for these qualities, as meaning something to people you know can help self-esteem.

- From this, you may find aspects of your personality of which you were previously unaware.

Self-awareness

To see oneself more clearly, it may help to find a common ground between positive and negative in terms of liking and valuing oneself.

- It is possible to be over positive about yourself, even to the extent that you can appear 'up yourself', which can distance you from others as well as from who you really are.

- At the other extreme, you can be over negative about yourself, to the extent where you are inflicting self-pity on yourself. Not only can this also distance you from others, but it can lead to an unmindful state, almost self-harming the mind.

- Being a little humble, without becoming up oneself or self-pitying extensively, may help you to see who you are more mindfully and to become more aware of how others may perceive you. Being 'humble' is just to be happy and content with who you are rather than over or downplaying it.

Encouraging confidence

There are numerous factors that can contribute to low self-esteem. Some suggestions for parents, professionals and others close to a person with Asperger's Syndrome to encourage self-esteem include:

- Don't compare a person with Asperger's Syndrome to others, as this can lead to low self-esteem by implying that 'someone else is better than you'.

- Try to encourage a person with Asperger's Syndrome to view their progress in relation to their own capabilities as an individual.

- Avoid sarcastic comments, as a person with Asperger's Syndrome might take them the wrong way and become upset.

CHAPTER 4

Seeing the Truth

How to control mind proliferation
and see others as they really are

Like others diagnosed with Asperger's Syndrome, I have experienced difficulty with flexible thinking, in terms of being able to look at different questions and issues from different perspectives. The Buddha's teachings suggest that just as the ears hear or the eyes see without any effort (unless blind and deaf), the mind also 'proliferates' thoughts almost effortlessly. Such thoughts can lead to various concepts that one may take delight in and cling onto thus taking them to be true. This process is known in Buddhism as proliferation of the mind (Papañca). In this chapter, I will look at the problems that holding onto one's opinions can create, and how opening up to other views can help one see the truth more closely and interpret it accordingly.

Tendency to 'cling' onto a view or opinion was often a problem for me when an undergraduate university student, as I often found myself believing my own Marxist-Leninist views over others. Though it isn't perhaps un-normal for university students to go through a 'left-wing' phase in relation to issues faced when university students, with me, it often appeared to my student colleagues to be a way for me to distance myself from them in terms of the way I interpreted it.

Marxism appealed to me when a student after I had read *The Communist Manifesto* for the first time and discovered left-wing orientated journals and magazines. The theories within Marxism that suggested society's wealth should be distributed evenly and should be based on the idea of 'each according to his ability, each according to his need' appealed to me after what I had been through at school, where many of my peers seemed to think that they were 'above' me in terms of the schoolyard pecking order. When a university student, I felt that I needed an 'identity' to go with where I was coming from in terms of my background. What I didn't realise though was that developing an identity for yourself, especially if politically or religiously motivated in a fundamental way, can be isolating.

I didn't realise it at the time, but developing strong views in relation to politics distanced me from others, and I perhaps came to be seen as predictable, in the sense that in conversation I would go over the same theme just about every time. My mind would cling to such views to the extent that I believed them to be the way, closing me to different perspectives. I found it very difficult to understand why others wouldn't agree with or accept my views, and also why others might develop different views.

I experienced many differences of opinion with others when a university student. I have since realised though that such differences often arose out of my own tendency to cling onto views that I felt comfortable with, as well as my not being able to understand why others wouldn't feel comfortable with my views. As a result, I often found myself in very one-sided conversations that sometimes ended up in heated verbal conflict.

Throughout my life, I have experienced fixations on and obsessions with different subjects, accumulating and retaining much knowledge each time. In some cases, I also developed strong opinions on different themes, including those where there is often no right or wrong answer. As a person with Asperger's Syndrome, I can still occasionally experience much confusion whenever this scenario occurs, especially when it involves having to make a decision.

When developing interests, it isn't unusual for me to start reading as much as possible about the subject of interest my attention has been drawn towards. The way my mind works, I still find it so easy to read so much and accumulate so much knowledge and information. However, not being able to 'read between the lines' and to interpret information with a more critical eye before processing it with a flexible mind means that I take it all literally. This has led me to directly believe adverts (in print and on television) and promotional literature as it is written, often without being sceptical of it, and often I have had to learn the hard way when I have bought a product that is made out to be so good, but I have ended up disappointed. This has happened to me with pursuing different courses in higher education, where I have believed qualifications to promise so much in terms of career prospects, but have been disappointed each time.

As well as having difficulty with one's own mind proliferation, many people with Asperger's Syndrome, including myself, can also have problems recognising the mind proliferation in others. This relates to difficulty that a person with Asperger's Syndrome can experience with flexible thinking, in terms of understanding why others may have different or extreme opinions, and how this can lead towards mind proliferation when one 'clings' onto such thought.

Around me in my day-to-day life there are many other individuals: those I know and see frequently, those whom I know but rarely see and those whom I hardly know. The increased self-awareness that I have developed from mind cultivation through meditation and experience of different cultures has helped me understand that all individuals have their own views and opinions, with it being more apparent in some than others. Sometimes though, when somebody clings onto a view, it can be very difficult for a person with Asperger's Syndrome to realise why the person concerned is likely to cling to that view. For myself, it can be especially difficult to understand if a view that someone clings to is either directed at me or relates to me in a more indirect way.

Often in my life, I have been oblivious to either being disliked or being seen as someone to avoid. I have been disliked at times for extreme opinions or ideas I have clung onto and been seen as someone to avoid in case I go off on a tangent about a subject on which I have a fixation, which when a student was often either politics or cricket. Being the way I am hasn't at times been acceptable to others in the sense that others have found my opinions, views, fixations and traits offensive, even if on my part any offence caused is largely unintentional. I have met other individuals diagnosed with Asperger's Syndrome who are often prone to similar experiences, many of which are due to difficulty with self-awareness.

It has often been the case that others have suggested that I am not good enough at doing something or don't have the necessary personal qualities in certain situations, particularly after the many job interviews I have been unsuccessful at. However, I have since learned to realise that it can often be the result of their mind proliferation, and that their interpretation may be different to those of others, who may see such situations differently. Believing the interpretations of yourself by others in this way can give them power, as others will think they can get you to support their views and opinions. One doesn't see who he or she really is when accepting others' opinions of who they are.

From my experience of different people from different backgrounds diagnosed with Asperger's Syndrome and their relations with those not on the autistic spectrum, I have found that some people can distance themselves from others, often by labelling – something that even I have been guilty of at times, particularly not long after diagnosis. Originating from autism e-mailing lists, people with Asperger's Syndrome often refer to one another as 'Aspies', and refer to those not on the spectrum as 'neuro-typical' (NT). The tendency among humans to label one another on the grounds of race, ethnicity, social class, etc. is well known, and sometimes individuals, including Aspies, consider themselves proud of their label whereas others may feel uncomfortable with it. Personally, I don't mind being referred to as an Aspie, but I have met other people diagnosed with Asperger's Syndrome who aren't so comfortable with the term, and have met people who aren't on the spectrum who aren't comfortable with the term NT. One has to be careful of using labels to set them apart from one another, as this can again result in divisions, which inevitably lead to conflict.

There are many people diagnosed with Asperger's Syndrome I have met who are, to some extent, proud of the term 'Aspie'. There is nothing wrong with being happy with who you are in such a way, as this can be a good thing in terms of personal happiness, particularly if knowing who you are in this way makes you more 'your own person'. However, I have seen it occur where those diagnosed with Asperger's Syndrome are so proud of the Aspie label that they find themselves attached to it to the extent that they cut themselves off from NTs. Though this is understandable if people diagnosed with Asperger's Syndrome feel they have been ill treated by NTs, the more that a person with Asperger's Syndrome distances him- or herself from NTs in this way, the less they will see others or themselves as they really are.

On the issue of relations between people diagnosed with autism or Asperger's Syndrome and those not on the autistic spectrum, something that I have learned since my diagnosis is the value of having close friends on the autistic spectrum and also those not on the spectrum. As well as becoming close friends with other people with Asperger's Syndrome who can relate well to me personally, I feel I have also benefited greatly from friends who are not on the autistic spectrum, including people I have worked and studied with, who, once they know me, have included me. Developing identities for oneself and for those one considers oneself different from can lead to experience of the hindrance of ill-will, as it can exclude others who don't fit such identities, leading potentially to heated conflict.

Through mind proliferation, we don't often see ourselves as we really are, and don't often see others as they really are. Often this is because one is unhappy or uncomfortable with who they are, and effectively 'edit' their vulnerabilities, often by clinging onto views or ideals that suit their strengths. There is nothing wrong with having views and opinions – I have views and opinions on provisions and services for people with autism and Asperger's Syndrome – but what one must be careful of is not to trust or be inflexible in them, as this can lead to non-acceptance of other people's opinions. One's own views and opinions, as with those of others, can be edited and we can gain very biased views about one another, including developing neurological prejudices, akin to prejudices on issues such as race, ethnicity and social class.

Mind proliferation is difficult for anybody to control effectively, not just for a person diagnosed with Asperger's Syndrome. Below are some suggestions for how one can exert control over this aspect of mind behaviour, to help see who they really are, and who others really are.

How to avoid excessive mind proliferation

The mind proliferates effortlessly, and it can take a lot of effort and training to control this tendency. Some suggestions for people with Asperger's Syndrome to keep mind proliferation in check include:

- It may help to be aware of potential consequences of holding onto a view or opinion – clinging onto a view or opinion without flexible thought can sow the seeds of conflict.

- Though it may be difficult, especially if you struggle with flexible thought, try to observe any views or opinions from other perspectives.

- It is natural, and not wrong, for one to have views and opinions, but if you feel that any view you have may offend, it may be better to keep it quiet.

How to recognise mind proliferation in others

Mind proliferation occurs in all of us, including people diagnosed with Asperger's Syndrome and those not on the autistic spectrum. To avoid being easily influenced by mind proliferation in others, it may help to recognise when one's own mind is proliferating:

- Views and opinions people hold may often relate to their personal experience, and so may not suit others.

- Try to avoid reacting angrily if you disagree with or are offended by another's view or opinion, as this can give power to others if they see you as vulnerable.

- If you disagree with or are offended by another's view or opinion, it may help to recognise the source of their mind proliferation.

How to understand sources of mind proliferation in people with Asperger's Syndrome

As many people with Asperger's Syndrome experience difficulty with flexible thinking, they may be susceptible to unintentionally offending or upsetting others through mind proliferation. For those who aren't on the autistic spectrum, to avoid conflict, it may help to:

- Recognise where possible that if a person with Asperger's Syndrome happens to offend through their opinions and views, it is more likely due to a difficulty with flexible thought rather than a deliberate attempt to offend.

- If a person with Asperger's Syndrome unintentionally offends in a social situation, try to avoid 'singling' the person out as bad or abusive. This can isolate the person with Asperger's Syndrome, making them feel they have been 'demonised', which can cause them much anxiety, especially if they haven't intended any such reaction.

- A person with Asperger's Syndrome can often be oblivious to why they may have offended another through their views or opinions. It may help to reassure the person with Asperger's Syndrome in this situation.

CHAPTER 5

Gaining Insight from Those Around Me

How insight can strengthen one's awareness

Finding that I had Asperger's Syndrome – a condition that I had never previously heard of – has taught me many things about myself that I didn't previously realise and that others could not have been aware of. From this, I feel that people close to me, including my family, can understand me much better. Partly through the practice of meditation, something else I feel that I have learned is to understand and appreciate the views and concerns of others, including people from my past.

Since publishing my autobiography, *Glass Half-Empty, Glass Half-Full* (Mitchell 2005), I have met some people from my past, including some of my former teachers. At times, when turning back the clock to what happened in my past, of the Five Hindrances, the one I often recognised was the second, ill-will, when I realised how many people there were with whom I could have been so angry! When reviewing my life so that I could write my life story, I spent much time revisiting my past. It wasn't easy at times to think about the more difficult times during my upbringing. But when thinking how I had been treated at times in my past, I realised how easy it would be for me to be nasty to a lot of people, especially those who bullied me in the schoolyard.

Though it was suggested in some reviews that there was some 'implied criticism' of how I was brought up, I didn't intend any criticism as such. What I felt needed to be understood though is the confusion that can result from growing up with undiagnosed Asperger's Syndrome. People around a person with undiagnosed Asperger's Syndrome, including members of their family, can experience frustration when they try so many different ideas to help the person develop social and independent skills with the best of intentions but have negative results. It is very easy in this way for a lot of people diagnosed with Asperger's Syndrome when adults, including myself, to feel that they were perhaps let down by various people who played a role in their upbringing.

From my upbringing of undiagnosed Asperger's Syndrome, perhaps one of the most important things I feel that I have learned regarding young people with Asperger's Syndrome is the importance of early diagnosis. Early diagnosis enables the right support to be available for both the person diagnosed with Asperger's Syndrome and those that matter in their upbringing (family, teachers, doctors, etc.), which can help them understand the condition and how it affects the individual. This can ultimately help remove the confusion and misunderstandings, together with any accusations of blame, so often remembered by people diagnosed with Asperger's Syndrome in later life, including myself.

However difficult it may be for any of us to forgive people from our past that have perhaps been unfair to us, an important life aspect I feel I have learned is how to look at people from my past as they are in the context of the present. This, in turn, allows people from my past to see me as I am now, as someone who has had to come to terms with difficult periods I have experienced. One of my former teachers, after reading my autobiography, said that he often got very angry and frustrated with himself for not being able to get through to me. After finding that he felt this way about me as his pupil, I realised that other teachers I had, as well as college/university lecturers and student colleagues, may well have experienced similar frustrations and confusions about me. Perhaps in some cases they may even have felt that such frustration hurt them emotionally almost as much as I felt hurt by the way they were towards me.

Many people who know me now view me and relate to me as I am now, being able to generally understand and appreciate the values and concerns of others, including being able to exercise sympathy and discretion where necessary. But when I was younger, I had much difficulty with being able to respond when questioned or spoken to by those involved in my upbringing. So often was this mistaken for ignorance that I wondered why I couldn't respond the way others assumed I would. I realise now how confused others must have been as to what to do to relate to me.

In this sense, being diagnosed with Asperger's Syndrome has been of great benefit not only to myself but also to those around me, so there is no need to feel frustrated about not being able to understand me. In this sense it can 'mask' the confusion that so often stands between an individual with undiagnosed or unknown Asperger's Syndrome and the world. During the months prior to my diagnosis in 1998, I was experiencing trauma and depression. When it was noticed that I was missing from lectures, some of my student colleagues got in touch with me to say that they all felt a little guilty in a way about how they had been with me.

In this way, a person who doesn't have Asperger's Syndrome can find out something about him- or herself through the way they relate to a person with Asperger's Syndrome, in terms of how they treat different people as individuals. Many people with Asperger's Syndrome, including myself and other individuals diagnosed with the condition I have met, often feel vulnerable socially, including being gullible and easily led. Something I have found is that, sometimes, a person with Asperger's Syndrome can almost be like an invisible 'acid test' for others in terms of how they treat different individuals with respect. A fictional example that I sometimes refer to to illustrate this is Roy Cropper from 'Coronation Street', the owner of 'Roy's Rolls' café. Roy appears to have traits associated with Asperger's Syndrome including a powerful memory to retain information relating to railways and historical figures, but is also very vulnerable to some of the more 'villainous' characters in terms of how they may exploit his apparent inadequacies. How a particular character treats Roy Cropper can often determine whether they are 'good' or 'evil'.

From the schoolyard through university, places of work and in some front-line services (e.g. banks, solicitors, estate agents), there is often evidence of social competition to which a person with Asperger's Syndrome can be vulnerable. Such social competition tactics, including bullying and belittling, tend to start off in the schoolyard as we have seen. As we get older though, such social competition is often still with us, but in different guises. As there is often so much social stigma attached to one's position within social hierarchies, some may try to project successful images through talking about how they may have a really nice house or flaunting their new expensive designer clothes, etc. Though in some working cultures, often when working in business, it may be necessary to project such an image of success towards clients. There are some who often use such tactics to attract those who aspire to success and exclude those they don't feel live up to their success. In some other cases, it could be that people try to project such an image to hide weaknesses.

Though others being aware of my Asperger's Syndrome diagnosis and how it affects me as an individual has helped in terms of understanding, there are still some aspects of me, I find, that sometimes aren't as apparent to others – my personal values. Occasionally, this has led to misunderstandings, especially when others have expectations of me that clash with what I value. Why my values can so often be misunderstood often arises from others thinking that I share similar life ambitions and goals, in terms of being driven by success and status. This kind of driving force though for me is often too stressful to manage in terms of anxiety, which is why I am generally happy just being content with a stable life. So, sometimes, I find it helpful to let colleagues know of my values to avoid them making such assumptions.

Insight meditation techniques, I feel, have helped me to be able to think more flexibly in the sense of being able to collect my thoughts when responding to others as well as being able to recognise the second hindrance of ill-will and how to undermine it more effectively. By seeing other people, from both my past and present, as they are now, I can generally become more tolerant, rather than holding grudges that develop to near uncontrollable friction. I have found that it helps to understand that those who bullied me in the schoolyard had problems of their own and former university colleagues who said I was an embarrassment to the class didn't perhaps know me well enough to understand why I made particular comments during seminars. When I meet people from my past, especially if it is someone with whom I experienced friction, I find that it helps to understand such sources of friction, often coming from their own difficulties or frustrations, and to be aware of these so I can see the person as they are now. In this way, I can extend my compassion towards them. But how others interpret me, is up to them.

To help develop more understanding of social relations for people with Asperger's Syndrome, including those being diagnosed when young and those diagnosed in later life, this is what I feel I have learned in relation to my own experience:

Importance of early diagnosis in social development

The earlier it is known that an individual is diagnosed with Asperger's Syndrome, the earlier it can be understood by others, especially those close to the individual. Here are some benefits of early diagnosis for parents/carers, professionals and teachers:

- Any accusations of blame in terms of not being able to understand the individual can be reduced.

- This can reduce pressure on the individual with Asperger's Syndrome.

- It can also reduce any confusion experienced with interpreting unknown Asperger's Syndrome.

How to respect others for a person with Asperger's Syndrome

To develop close relations, personal and working, it often helps to look at people around you as they are now, whatever they may have been like to you in the recent past:

- Focusing on past instances can reopen old wounds, which can lead to further friction and formation of grudges, which can preoccupy the mind leading to taking actions without thinking.

- People from your past, especially if they knew you prior to diagnosis and perhaps misunderstood or mistreated you, rather than displaying apathy may feel guilty or frustrated about not being able to relate to you.

- However, there may also be people from your past who show apathy and find personal thrill from exercising control over others. In this case, it may be best to avoid them, as reacting can give them power, especially if it shows you are weak.

How to make your values known without causing friction

As an individual with Asperger's Syndrome, your values and concerns may often be very different from those of your colleagues. If so, they may not be very apparent to your colleagues. Sometimes, if you feel it necessary, it may help to make your values known:

- Look at what you do – Observe yourself and how you act in relation to those around you, including how you treat others. Allow complete honesty over reasons you have in mind for why you took one action over another.

- Ask others for feedback – Find out what others, in particular those close to you, think you may value.

- Reflect – Bring together findings from your feedback and find out how your values relate to what others expect of you. If your values differ from what others expect of you, make it clear that your values are real through your behaviour.

How to be mindful of and respect individuals diagnosed with Asperger's Syndrome

As described, it is easy to feel guilty for mistreating a person with Asperger's Syndrome through lack of understanding. To reduce such guilt, some advice for others to relate to and respect an individual with Asperger's Syndrome includes:

- Remember that all individuals diagnosed with Asperger's Syndrome are different in terms of personality and characteristics. In this sense it may help to treat a person with Asperger's Syndrome as an individual.

- Try not to think of a person with Asperger's Syndrome as being disabled or broken, as this may appear controlling or patronising.

- Where you can, allow the person with Asperger's Syndrome to be 'who they are' in an informal conversation. Though the person with Asperger's Syndrome may struggle or misunderstand social gestures, such as when to stop talking, it is often much easier to be generous to a misunderstanding than explicitly point it out. After all, we can all have them.

CHAPTER 6

Worrying in
an Anxiety-driven World

How to curb tendency to worry through curtailing stress and anxiety

Anxiety is present in some shape or form almost every day in our lives. As a person with Asperger's Syndrome, I have experienced much difficulty in being able to cope with anxiety, to the extent that it has taken over my mind. When a particular anxiety issue arises, such as uncertainty over whether my contract is going to be renewed or whether retail, petrol or utility bill prices are going to rise or generally not knowing what lies ahead, I can hear playbacks in my mind, almost like having a tape recorder inside my head. For me this is often difficult to curtail. In this case, the fourth hindrance of restlessness and worry represents the interference that leads to such difficulties. Inability to recognise and curtail 'mind blockages' that arise from the fourth hindrance can in turn lead to further mind blockages associated with the second hindrance of ill-will towards oneself and others.

As I described in *Glass Half-Empty, Glass Half-Full* (Mitchell 2005), I have experienced much anxiety relating to educational and social issues. When one of the reviews described me as having difficulty with an inflexible education system, I realised that my education from school through to university was largely based on my chronological age rather than my mental age in terms of how under-developed my social skills perhaps were then. The way I see it, for most of us, life starts to turn from upbringing to becoming driven by the forces of anxiety and pressure when we reach the ages of 13 to 14, when our lives start to 'matter' in terms of decisions we make and, in some cases, expectations of attainment. Relating to this, Dr Rowan Williams, the Archbishop of Canterbury, in 2006 said in an interview that teenagers' lives are becoming increasingly anxiety-driven as they don't have a year that is free from testing in some shape or form.

In such an atmosphere, one can feel very vulnerable, especially a person with Asperger's Syndrome. Those around the individual with Asperger's Syndrome are likely to experience similar anxieties and frustrations but it may not be as apparent as they may find a way of dealing with it, sometimes at the expense of a person with Asperger's Syndrome. Growing up during teenage years is often about asserting superiority over your peers as a reaction to being controlled and told what to do by adults, usually parents and teachers. Often, such competition for superiority can result in emotional issues, including depression, feelings of inferiority and bullying. This is why I don't really lay blame to those who made my school life difficult.

Such anxiety that drives our teenage years continues into adult life, by which time most of us have experienced these kinds of emotional issues as teenagers. People with Asperger's Syndrome, especially if they have led very sheltered lives as teenagers like I did, often haven't experienced such a period of social and emotional maturation that marks the transition into adulthood. So some people with Asperger's Syndrome may experience emotional issues in their twenties that most experience in their teens. I for one feel that this sort of life pattern still affects me now in terms of my social development. But as the general consensus in our society suggests, an individual is an adult when he or she is 18 years old, but this isn't often the case with a person with Asperger's Syndrome. Very rarely does one's chronological age match their mental age. Quite often, support in dealing with issues such as anxiety is needed well into adult life.

As an adult with Asperger's Syndrome, anxiety issues I have faced have often related to uncertainty. For instance, my working life for a few years was largely spent working on contract-based arrangements, which were rarely renewed, and each time I found myself having to look for work again. For me, working to these kinds of arrangements led to a lot of anxiety over the uncertainty of my immediate future, especially since I didn't know if there was still a job for me once my contract came to an end, with the added stress of having to look for a new job, often involving going through mountains of application forms. Added to the anxiety, this process each time saw me experience mental overload, rather like a computer experiencing e-mail overload. Rather than crashing though, I often found myself becoming very bitter and even twisted.

Looking back, the anxiety that plagued me during those years took control of me to the extent that it was even affecting the quality of my work. For often, when I felt that my mind was troubled by such uncertainty, it was so difficult for me to focus on the immediate task in hand. When having to try and balance these particular concerns, I often found that my mind ended up reacting to situations and in some cases certain people in a quite cynical way. This was where my inability to recognise the fourth hindrance of restlessness and worry verged into the second hindrance of ill-will towards myself and others.

When looking for work, something that I often find myself having to question is whether a particular role is going to be heavily varied or unpredictable. Having to respond to unpredictable situations for me involves having to collect my thoughts and to think quickly, which I struggle to do. When I have to go through this process, I often end up having to take actions without thinking, and it is still very difficult for me to realise the consequences of those actions including the potential impact they may have on others. Doing something like this would mentally hurt me as much as the people whom the action affects, particularly as I don't consider myself as the type who gains thrill or pleasure from such control over the lives of others, including the power to almost play with people's lives and even their emotions. These are among many reasons why I found that a career in the newspaper industry wasn't suitable for me.

Where I have been happiest at work is in jobs that are largely based around routine and general predictability, and most importantly, are stable. I am not saying that I am unable to cope with, or that other individuals with Asperger's Syndrome are unable to cope with, changes in routine, and I am aware that changes in routine do happen. When most of my working tasks and duties are routine, though not necessarily simple, this enables me to manage change more effectively without much stress and anxiety, as long as I am informed of any potential changes that may occur.

Away from working hours, where I can sometimes experience anxiety is with financial issues, finding my way round a place I am not used to (whether walking, driving or via public transport) and any situations that generally involve uncertainty. When I can't know or anticipate potential outcomes, anxiety can take over my mind.

Other situations in which feelings of worry and anxiety can take over my mind are those that involve waiting for an outcome that may determine my immediate or long-term future. Such issues include waiting for the outcome of a job interview or for an exam or test result. Worry over what the outcome may be for me still encourages me to sometimes hide from it rather than accept it. Perhaps the kinds of situations where I can still experience anxiety and worry more so than others are situations that you can't plan or revise for. If I am able to anticipate certain situations that may arise, I am usually able to handle them appropriately, but for those where I can't anticipate, it is still very difficult for me to collect and cultivate my thoughts.

Usually, to try and avoid encountering awkward or unpredictable situations, it helps me to plan. This is particularly important when travelling, so that I don't miss train or flight times, as it is often difficult for me to work out an alternative route on the spot. I experience so much confusion which turns into anxiety over railway ticketing arrangements in terms of there being so many ticket types and prices for similar journeys. It also frustrates me that railway ticket arrangements in the UK are so confusing to me as I usually enjoy the experience of travelling by train!

It is often confusing for me that one of my favourite pastimes – travelling – can also be a source of anxiety for me. I enjoy travelling for many different reasons, whether for historical or cultural interest in a particular place or for scenery. But I can only really enjoy it without having to experience so much anxiety. This is why when I travel I tend to go on all-inclusive organised tours, so that I am able to visit different and varied places of interest within a planned itinerary, so I don't have to worry about booking tickets or hotels while on the move.

Samatha meditation techniques, I feel, have gradually enabled me to retain a calm state of mind, which has helped me handle situations where I would have perhaps otherwise experienced excessive feelings of anxiety and worry. When I do experience anxiety and worry, I am able to bring the calm states of mind that I experience during Samatha practice into the situation, so that I am able to handle it in a more relaxed way, letting it slowly pass by. I find that generally stepping back from it all through meditation or undertaking a physical activity (e.g. walking) or even doing a routine job (e.g. washing the dishes, vacuuming) helps to put such feelings aside so that I can handle them appropriately when I need to.

Problems with worrying

Something that many people with Asperger's Syndrome appear to be good at is worrying, which only adds to anxiety, crippling your mind's capacity for effective thinking to overcome it. Problems excessive worrying can create include:

- Worrying can show weakness, which can give power to others who may exploit it.

- You may find through excessive worrying that you forget to eat and lose your appetite without noticing, resulting in skipping meals.

- Excessive worrying may also lead to social isolation.

Curtailing anxiety

If you feel anxiety is troubling you, you may feel as though you just don't want to do anything. By doing nothing, you may find your levels of anxiety increasing. Instead, it is often good to step back from the anxiety by doing something different. Undertaking a different task, whether it is washing dishes or cutting grass, if it is separate from your worries, may help balance your thought process. Some suggestions for an individual with Asperger's Syndrome to ease anxiety include:

- Exercise may be a good way for some to curtail worrying thoughts. Focusing your body on something may put your mind at ease.

- Try to avoid skipping meals, so that your appetite is satisfied and you don't feel the need to 'snack' every so often.

- Where you can, it may help to develop or renew intimacies with friends and family. Such closeness can bring insight and relieve agitation and depression.

Curtailing stress

Stress is another factor that may lead to anxiety. Stress can come courtesy of pressure and being overloaded with tasks or duties. One only has so much energy available, which may need to be re-concentrated every so often. To reduce stress it may help to:

- Where possible, try to take life in moderation, ascertain what you feel you need in life, and slowly begin to balance work with relaxation.

- Try to identify the aspects of your life that demand the most work and energy. Prioritise the essential aspects and leave time to focus on the non-essential. This will enable you to work towards alleviating pressure and conserving your time and energy, feeling more centred.

- If you feel you are being 'put upon' in terms of taking on extra responsibilities in a working environment, it may help to try and set a limit with your supervisor as to allocated workload. Alternatively, if you are studying and need extra time with assignments due to other responsibilities in life, try to negotiate an extension – after all one can only do so much.

CHAPTER 7

Curtailing Feelings of Anger and Frustration

How to control and respond to anger effectively

As discussed in the previous chapter, one of the emotions that anxiety can create is frustration, which can lead to anger. There are many issues regarding certain aspects of my own life that can make me very angry, including being unsuccessful at job interviews, and in some cases certain comments people might say to me. Looking at the bigger picture, there are numerous other, often very different, issues that make other individuals angry, depending on their personalities and values. Where the previous chapter discussed how inability to recognise the fourth hindrance of restlessness and worry sometimes verges into the second hindrance of ill-will towards oneself and others, this chapter looks at the effect that the second hindrance can have for an individual with Asperger's Syndrome, including how anger expressed by others at a person with Asperger's Syndrome can lead to ill-will on both sides.

In many different social hierarchies, such as educational establishments or workplaces, there are often pressures that feed down from one level to the next, almost like a 'chain reaction'. For instance, a school pupil with Asperger's Syndrome may feel upset or hurt by a teacher's comment about their work or behaviour. Similarly, a university student with Asperger's Syndrome may feel hurt by feedback given by tutors criticising their work or their progress generally. What may be very difficult for the person with Asperger's Syndrome to recognise though, particularly if they have difficulty in being able to recognise the source of the hindrance, is why a teacher or employer may be angry with them. For instance, teachers under pressure to achieve results (e.g. in inspections, league tables) may exert their frustration on their students, and employers who have to meet certain service targets or quality thresholds (e.g. applying for Charter Mark, ISO), including meeting the expectations of clients, and may exert such frustrations on their employees for 'not trying hard enough'. Such issues can be difficult for a student or employee diagnosed with Asperger's Syndrome to recognise, especially if they have difficulty in being able to cope with such anxiety and frustration.

When I was a university student, it happened to me on some occasions that I failed an exam by around 3–5 per cent. When I felt frustrated at having just missed out on passing, something one of my tutors said was that '3 per cent is a huge margin of failure in terms of standards expected'. Such comments didn't only add to my frustration but also made me very angry. I became angry with the tutor who said this and that anger gradually took over my mind to the extent that I became very angry with the whole set-up at university.

Like many other people with Asperger's Syndrome, I have also had much trouble being able to find employment, having been unsuccessful at so many interviews, either when looking for a new post if unemployed or facing potential unemployment or looking for a promotion. Many times after being unsuccessful at job interviews, I have become very angry. But each time after becoming angry and frustrated at not being able to make the breakthrough, the anger has so often got to me that it has hurt my determination to keep trying, and I have lost my focus.

For most of us, it is natural to feel frustrated and angry going through the process of looking for work but not finding it, especially if you need a job for financial reasons. For many other disappointments that a person with Asperger's Syndrome may experience, there are often remedies and releases to put it aside, but if you are trying to come to terms with the disappointment of being turned down for a particular job that you really want and then find more letters of rejection coming through the post, it can be soul-destroying.

As a person with Asperger's Syndrome who has been through this process, I have found that the more frustrated and angrier that it has made me, the more it has detached my mind from my body, in that the mind loses much bodily control, including control of the nervous system, leading to tension and shaking. When my mind is elsewhere, I can lose both awareness and control over the body in the sense that I find myself thinking about something different to what I am supposed to be doing, such as putting in the wrong ingredients when cooking. This has resulted in me at times becoming very angry for very irrational reasons, which have led me to blame so many others for my problems rather than myself.

One of the main problems I find with becoming very angry is that you can shut yourself off from others around you, including those close to you. When most of us find ourselves involved in a heated argument or have had a major disagreement with someone, we may understandably feel it necessary to talk to someone about it the moment after. Though it is a good idea to talk about problems with someone whom you may feel understands, after you have just had a heated argument, your mind is often still so full of anger that you think only of yourself and how your issue or dispute affects you. So when you tell someone else about it, what you often find yourself doing is editing it to exclude the other person's point of view to make it sound as though it's all somebody else's fault and not yours in any way at all.

I often found myself going through this during very diffi-cult times at school, university or when unemployed. For instance, when at university, I found myself becoming so angry with the whole environment, even to the extent of being angry with and blaming people who weren't even remotely involved with my studies and in some cases blaming people that didn't even exist. When I was unemployed after already having been through the soul-destroying process of having been rejected by many potential employers, I became angry with people who had been taken on instead of me and with all representatives on interview panels that had interviewed me. When being angry with those who had been taken on for a job that I particularly wanted, I felt that there was so much for me to be angry about, such as that the person who was taken on didn't have as good qualifications as I had.

These particular problems that I have experienced with anger are examples of where it can detach one from reality. At university or when unemployed, when I ran out of people to be angry with, the only person for me to be angry with was myself. As my mind was by then detached from my body, I didn't care any more about my physical health, which led to self-harm. Fortunately though, I was able to get out of it quickly, before the effects of it on my physical health could have been worse.

As well as being able to manage and cope with one's own anger, we are all capable, directly or indirectly, of making other people angry. From my own anger, something that I have found is that it can give power to those you are angry with, some of whom may use this to their advantage to put you into more dif-ficult circumstances. For many people with Asperger's Syndrome, including myself, it can often be difficult to realise what can potentially make others angry or how the conse-quences of their actions can make a person or group of people angry. Different individuals can become angry for numerous different reasons, including very trivial ones. Those familiar with autism literature will no doubt know how well documented it is that many people with Asperger's Syndrome struggle with social interaction through inability to understand the unwritten rules associated with it. One of the aspects of this inability though is not being aware of what, however minor, can indirectly make somebody angry. But equally, others may not understand the values of or be aware of a person diagnosed with Asperger's Syndrome and how actions they take, including what they say, can make the person with Asperger's Syndrome angry.

Sometimes though, anger can be justified, especially if it is directed towards correcting injustice. As a person with Asperger's Syndrome, I have experienced such anger in relation to my feelings on how services and provision for adults with Asperger's Syndrome are largely non-existent, how many adults with Asperger's Syndrome may have good skills and qualifications but can't use them, not to mention how many experience much difficulty in being able to obtain employment. But what I have found is that for anger to have any kind of effect or impact it must be channelled appropriately.

It has happened to me a number of times where after being turned down for a job, failing a test, etc. I have had an immediate outburst of rage. This occurred many times while at university, where I had such an outburst over not getting as high grades as others, especially after feeling I had put in more work, or each time I failed my driving test when there were so many others already driving often doing things that they would fail their test on (e.g. incorrect signals when coming back to the inside lane). But being angry not only made the situation worse for me, but made things worse for others around me, especially those close to me, as it became difficult for others to help me, especially my family. Looking back, it was like me wielding a sword with a blade on each end in terms of the anger I was experiencing. The blade on the end nearest to those I was angry with was distancing them from me, whilst the blade facing me was emotionally hurting me further.

A strategy I have since learned to prevent me from distancing myself from others through exerting anger excessively is to exert it behind closed doors, so that I can come to terms with what I am angry about without interference. I have also found that expressing anger can be one's own 'edited' version of events, a creation of the mind. This is where one can become almost Teflon-coated, throwing accusations and blame at others while none sticks to them.

Ajahn Munindo (2005), senior abbot at Aruna Ratanagiri Monastery in Harnham, Northumberland, suggests that, though one can feel 'better' by having someone or something else to blame, by blaming, one is only making more enemies, leading to further anger through insecurity. This can be difficult for a person with Asperger's Syndrome to realise when they are angry, and it can also be difficult to realise this when other people are angry with them. Laying blame both ways, the two parties involved can experience suffering. The party on the receiving end of the blaming can experience low self-esteem, but the party applying the blame often makes enemies, a different kind of suffering.

People not on the autistic spectrum are just as likely to get angry with a person with Asperger's Syndrome as a person with Asperger's Syndrome is likely to get angry with them. Here are some suggestions on how to control anger for people with Asperger's Syndrome, and how to respond to anger directed at them, and, for all parties, how to avoid applying blame.

Problems with anger

Some of the problems that excessive anger can create include:

- Anger can make you vulnerable to social isolation.

- Being angry can lead to regrettable actions, including emotional hurt inflicted on others as well as physical damage of precious items.

- Anger can give power to those that you are angry with, who may use it to their advantage against you or exploit you.

How to cope with anger effectively

Sometimes it may feel necessary to express anger to exhaust it from one's mind – this is often best done behind closed doors. Some suggestions for a person with Asperger's Syndrome on how to express and control anger effectively include:

- Sometimes, when angry, one may find him- or herself taking regrettable actions, including damaging items perhaps dear to oneself or to others. If feel you need to express your anger physically, it may be necessary to use an instrument or apparatus designed for physical impact (e.g. punch bag).

- When angry, you are not often in control of your own mind, including how your mind may relate to others, especially if you have had a major disagreement or heated argument with someone. It may be necessary to spend some time by yourself before taking further action, either pursuing an unrelated task or engaging in some form of entertainment (comedy or humour may be a good remedy for some) to give your mind a break.

- If you are angry about something or with someone, it may be worth trying to put such anger across diplomatically, as this can distance you from those who you are angry with, and chances are they won't cooperate or listen otherwise.

How to respond to anger effectively

Many people with Asperger's Syndrome can find themselves being on the receiving end of another's anger, not often realising what they may have done to cause the anger. When faced with anger, it may help to:

- Try to avoid 'back-biting' or responding to anger with anger, as this can show vulnerability.

- Remember that the person or party that is angry with you is likely to direct their anger from their own edited version of circumstances, needing someone to blame while papering over their own faults.

- Where possible, try to understand the source of their anger, so that you are able to rectify the circumstances where you can.

How to curtail anger and avoid attaching blame

Attaching blame can often be a result of acting on one's anger. It helps to curtail the anger first, by not acting on it, before doing something one may regret. This can allow for a more considerate approach when dealing with the issue that has made you angry. Suggestions for both people with Asperger's Syndrome and those not on the autistic spectrum:

- To avoid acting upon anger, it may help to undertake an activity or task unrelated to the circumstances that have made you angry (e.g. physical exercise, going for a run/walk) before reviewing the circumstances concerned with a clearer mind.

- When reviewing the circumstances, consider your own part in them as well as those whom you have made angry, as this may help you avoid applying blame under false pretences.

- Try to be mindful of the potential consequences of 'blaming', including the long-term effects it may have, such as making enemies.

CHAPTER 8

Discipline and Routine

How to maintain discipline within routine, including managing changes

I experienced difficulties with the lack of structured routine when at university as well as during my school years when much of my time away from school was spent alone in my room. More recently, when working as an academic research assistant, a role run purely off one's own time management, I often became very confused as to when to even start or finish, let alone when to take a break for lunch. As a person with Asperger's Syndrome, I feel I need routine to reduce high-level anxiety, but often though, to keep that routine, one needs the self-discipline to keep it in check. In this chapter, I will focus on how meditation practice together with belief can enable self-discipline.

The depression that I experienced prior to my diagnosis of Asperger's Syndrome in 1998 was, I now feel, partly the result of loss of self-discipline, which then led to a loss of routine in which I felt comfortable. When losing routine, I found myself developing some unhealthy habits. Fortunately, such habits didn't extend to dangerous ones such as drugs and alcohol, but my eating pattern became unhealthy in that I wasn't eating proper meals. Instead, I found myself snacking on foods such as biscuits and crisps. My mind had become so full of anxiety to the extent that I often didn't realise I was hungry and lost a lot of weight as a result.

Trying to get some sleep was also very difficult for me during this troubled time, due to the anxiety I felt I was facing over my future after university, over where I would be living in the next few years, whether I would be able to find work after university and other related issues. Each time I needed sleep, my mind just couldn't switch off and I would find myself tired the next day. Not giving myself enough to eat, I had little energy to do much. Being unsure of where I would go after university, I had begun to wonder what the point of a university education was and I began to lose the discipline to put in the effort needed to complete my degree. Losing discipline, I felt, came courtesy of experience of the fifth hindrance, doubt, which in turn became high-level third hindrance, sloth and torpor.

Why I often found it so difficult to establish a routine in which I was comfortable at university as a student and later as an academic research assistant was the lack of a set timetabled environment. Often, when a university student, particularly if in the final year of a course, very little time is spent in lectures and seminars during the course of a week, as the rest of the time is supposed to be used for researching and writing essays, planning and developing projects, etc. As an academic research assistant, other than occasional meetings and conferences, there is virtually no timetable at all. Everything is done off one's own time management. In this role, like I had done when a university student, I again found myself snacking rather than eating meals, as I was often confused about when to take lunch. But the biggest source of anxiety I often experienced as a research assistant was with whether or not my contract was going to be renewed every six months.

Fortunately, such losses of discipline and routine didn't extend long term, but could have done very easily without my own motivation to regain them. One of the many benefits I feel I have gained from meditation practice and belief is that it has given me routine in terms of setting aside time each day to practise. The practice itself I feel has given me the discipline to maintain a routine in which I am comfortable, which reduces my anxiety levels. To realise the potential benefits that meditation can have, one must apply the right effort and concentration to actually go through with the practice. Such input can then be transferred to other situations where right effort and concentration is needed, from very simple tasks such as copy-typing a letter to completing a long-term project.

One of the most useful necessities I feel that a belief or religion, be it Buddhism, Christianity, Islam, Judaism, etc., can give one is self-discipline, important for one's conduct in their daily life. As a lay Buddhist, or one who takes refuge in the Buddha who isn't part of the monastic community, I have five precepts:

1. abstaining from injury to living beings

2. abstaining from taking what is not given

3. abstaining from misconduct concerning sense pleasures

4. abstaining from false speech

5. abstaining from unmindful states due to alcoholic drink or drugs.

Rather than being rules to abide by, I view them as guidelines to 'adapt' to, according to my daily living pattern in relation to my immediate surroundings, including working environment and home life.

Many of the issues I have discussed so far relate to my past, but I feel I need discipline and routine in many different aspects of daily life, so that I am able to exercise awareness and control over them to reinforce my need for predictability in my life, which in turn reduces anxiety. Together with meditation, belief also helps in relation to the five precepts I have as one who takes refuge in the Buddha, to which I can adapt my needs as a person with Asperger's Syndrome.

One of the aspects of daily life where I feel that development of effective self-discipline has been of help is in management of money. Many people who know me know that I have never really been a big or reckless spender, instead, for much of my adult life I have been known for being 'too tight'. Such tightness with money relates to difficulties I have experienced in being able to obtain employment, thus not being paid a salary, and even when in employment, my income has often been in the lower regions. Perhaps more so though, my money-tightness is related to fear, including fear of either being ripped off or conned and of being in debt, including the possibility of personal bankruptcy. It has become the norm in recent years to hear stories in the news about how consumer debt in the UK is very high and what people face in terms of how they have to go about repaying it. Becoming attached to such fears had for a while made me over-zealous about spending money, to the extent where I wouldn't spend even on what I needed, such as food and clothing.

To help manage money in a disciplined way so that I am able to remain financially secure and have enough to spend on small, occasional luxuries, I find it helpful, when budgeting, to allocate 'chunks' of my salary to what I need to pay, such as utility bills and car insurance, and work out how much I can put away into savings for the future. When considering buying things for whatever reason, such as when needing new clothes, or buying a book or CD for personal enjoyment, I find it helpful for a small voice to come into my mind saying 'think'. When buying something such as a new camera, new clothes or a holiday, I consider what I will gain from it both short and long term, so that if I am short of money, I then consider if I really need what it is I have been looking at. This, I feel, enables me to stretch my salary.

Previously, when being overcautious about spending money, I would also develop what I now call 'financophobia', where I would hide from finances, not looking at my bank balance when displayed on a withdrawal receipt or bank statement. With access to online banking and with increased awareness, I find it much less of a phobia to hide from my finances, and know how much I can spend. These days, I now find it helpful to be aware of how much money I have, but not to let it be a concern, as I feel I have developed the discipline to handle it appropriately so that I am able to stay financially secure but also use it wisely, including treating others occasionally.

As well as with finance, self-discipline has also been helpful for me in terms of eating and drinking patterns. Though I have, fortunately, never succumbed to the excess of drugs and alcohol, I can see how easy a route it can be to go down for many people with Asperger's Syndrome, including some I know personally, who have felt so let down by life that they develop a craving to escape its grim reality. Self-discipline, I find, can be a useful tool in terms of controlling such cravings. Though one of the five precepts I have as one who takes refuge in the Buddha says that 'I will undertake the rule of training to abstain from unmindful states due to alcoholic drink or drugs', I find that with mindfulness, I am able to take in the occasional glass of wine without letting it develop into a craving, so that I don't intoxicate myself.

As I have previously mentioned in this chapter, I have often experienced cravings for snacking when faced with uncertainty. This has often been because my mind has been so preoccupied by the uncertainty that I am not awakened to my nourishment needs. To the other extent, when I know I am hungry and start eating, I sometimes find it very difficult to know when my appetite is satisfied. This often used to occur at events where there was a buffet service on or at an 'all you can eat' restaurant where, especially if I felt very hungry, I felt I needed to eat as much as I could before realising that my appetite was satisfied and usually ended up with indigestion.

Experiencing the monastic lifestyle staying at Aruna Ratanagiri Monastery in Harnham, Northumberland, one of the guidelines for monastic living that I was subject to was only eating 'solid' foods at certain times of the day: breakfast from 6 a.m.–7 a.m. and meal offering from 11 a.m.–12 noon. The food available in a Buddhist monastery in a Western country is alms food donated and cooked on site by the lay community, which one living the monastic lifestyle in the Theravāda tradition must accept to avoid being fussy over choice of what to eat, and also realise the need of eatable food to sustain one's body, rather than to indulge in pleasure.

I have often been first to admit that I am 'particular' about what I eat as well as having various favourite meals, and have often tended to stick with the same food choices rather than varying my diet. But after a period of hard work tidying Aruna Ratanagiri's gardens, through mindfulness I realised that I needed food to sustain the body and felt hungry enough to eat whatever eatable food was being offered during the meal offering, but being mindful of the monastic conditions, I also felt it necessary to take only what I needed when offered food, so that there was enough for other visitors to eat. Observing the guidelines regarding mealtimes helped me to realise the value of being open to different food than I may otherwise choose, helping me become used to a varied and disciplined diet.

With mindfulness, I find that I am able to notice more easily when my appetite is satisfied, so that I don't need to overeat, and it enables me to have more discipline over my eating patterns as well as being more open to a varied diet. With favourite foods, over-indulgence in pleasure of its taste can lead to one wanting more of the same, not realising when overeating that the hindrance of sense desire takes over one's mindfulness. I am still able to like my favourite foods and meals (e.g. steak, chips, chocolate), but I am mindful of what eating too much of them can do and know how much is enough. Mindfulness, I find, can help one be aware of how you feel bodily in terms of not only recognising when full up, but also helping to effectively gauge how much food you *need* to fill up before noticing the feeling later.

As well as helping with personal responsibility, discipline gained through meditation practice can also give one key disciplines in terms of personal development, including how one relates to their surroundings. When a child, I could often be hyperactive, and even now as an adult I still occasionally feel an urge to make movements, such as shaking my arms and fingers, which seem weird to others. To practise meditation, the purpose is for the body to stay still. Bringing this discipline into daily life enables me to remain still and calm when required.

Another discipline needed in meditation is attention, focusing particularly on the breath, and what stage of breath I am in. Sometimes, particularly when in a counting stage, I may find myself doing a longer breathing count when I am supposed to be in a shorter breathing count. Alternatively, when in a following, touching or settling stage, I can find myself counting! To curb this, it helps me to call back my wandering mind and pay attention. Again, this is a discipline that I can incorporate into activities and situations in my life where attention is needed, including being able to listen attentively when someone else is speaking, which is of particular importance when learning a new skill.

People diagnosed with Asperger's Syndrome are often described as liking routine. Though this is often true in the sense that many people with the condition, including myself, perhaps like routine because they experience much anxiety over change, it isn't to say that people with Asperger's Syndrome don't welcome changes in their routine. Where I find I sometimes struggle with change is adjusting to it, especially if it is sudden, but as long as I can manage it appropriately, I can assess any benefits it may have.

The Buddha's teachings suggest that one of the sources of dukkhā relates to impermanence in our lives. Something that I have found in today's highly competitive job market, is that even a permanent post isn't entirely secure, especially in situations where managers are having to make savings almost every financial year, which affect employees. Having been affected by this in recent years working in local government, where authorities are seemingly having to deliver more with less staff, I have found it helpful to, where possible, anticipate where change may occur, so that I can prepare for it.

Though routine is a good thing in the sense that it gives one discipline and stability, it can also be a source of dukkhā, especially if one becomes attached to it. As many people with Asperger's Syndrome may understandably feel comfortable in a particular routine, it is helpful, I find, to be mindful that such routines are impermanent, and will thus be more than likely subject to change. Though one can't easily forecast as and when change may arise, being aware of its possibility, without transcending into worry or even fear of it, can avoid attachment to routine, and thus enable one to anticipate and manage change effectively and, in some cases, maybe even welcome it. In my own ever-varying life, change is something that I have learned can be welcome and even rewarding.

Developing discipline

Discipline is essential to help one get through a day's work or study from waking up in the morning. Alternatively, if not in work or study, it may also help one to make the best of the situation, however difficult or unpleasant. Here are some suggestions on how to develop self-discipline:

- Try not to see tasks or duties as 'chores', as this can lead to negative states of mind. Instead, try to look at tasks you do at work or during study in a positive way, including what successful completion of them can enable.

- If you are unfortunate not to be in work or study, you can easily find yourself in a 'rut'. To develop and keep a routine, it may help to find an activity (e.g. voluntary work in the community, gardening, art), as this can help take you away from negative mental states.

- Time management is often difficult for people with Asperger's Syndrome to grasp, and deadlines can contribute to anxiety. It may also help though to see a deadline for completion of a task as a motivating factor to undertake the work, otherwise one may put it to one side, forgetting about it.

Finding routine

Self-discipline is often good for enabling routine, which can provide stability and reduce anxiety. Though routine is often reassuring for people with Asperger's Syndrome, it can also be a source of frustration and even anger if faced with change, given its impermanent nature.

- Try to see routine as a guideline rather than an itinerary or schedule.

- Where possible, try to adapt a routine you feel most comfortable in to different environments, especially if you are changing jobs.

- To avoid getting attached to routine, it may be necessary to make occasional subtle changes to your day-to-day life, such as taking lunch breaks at a different time, taking a different route to university or work. This can help adjusting to change when needed easier.

Preparing for change

Though a person with Asperger's Syndrome may experience much anxiety over change, it doesn't necessarily mean that they dislike it. Difficulties with coping with change may be more to do with difficulty in being able to anticipate changes likely to affect them. Some suggestions to help a person with Asperger's Syndrome anticipate and adjust to change include:

- If you manage or supervise a person with Asperger's Syndrome in work/study, don't automatically assume they are aware of or able to anticipate changes likely to affect them. It may help to inform them of any potential changes in their respective work/study environment so that they are aware of them.

- Encourage the person with Asperger's Syndrome to grasp new skills, procedures, etc. before change comes into effect so they can manage the transition effectively.

- Find out from the person with Asperger's Syndrome if there is anything (e.g. any training) they may need to manage forthcoming changes.

CHAPTER 9

Developing Tolerance

How to develop acceptance of and openness towards others without resorting to naivety

In Chapter 4, I discussed how holding onto a view or opinion can be the root of conflict. As well as creating such divisions through holding onto views, strong disagreement can also be a factor in conflict. In this chapter I will explore how one can accept others, even if they disagree with one's views and opinions, through tolerance, including how those diagnosed with Asperger's Syndrome can tolerate different individuals with the condition, as well as how those not on the autistic spectrum and people with Asperger's Syndrome can become tolerant of one another.

One of the uplifting joys that I have experienced meeting many other individuals diagnosed with Asperger's Syndrome is finding that all people on the autistic spectrum are different. Though in some cases we share some similarities, no two of us are the same. We are all different in terms of characteristics, intelligence, interests and levels of mindfulness. It could be said that people on the autistic spectrum are even more different as individuals among themselves than people who aren't on the spectrum.

When speaking or writing about Asperger's Syndrome, one of the things that I advocate is the availability of and access to social groups, as this not only aids development of social skills, but also opens one up to others' experiences of Asperger's Syndrome and related conditions. Though there are many others diagnosed with Asperger's Syndrome, including my friends Garry Burge and Tara Kimberley Torme, whose stories of how they came to be diagnosed have parallels with my own, there are others I have met whose stories are very different.

From meeting so many other individuals diagnosed with Asperger's Syndrome, something I have found is that the condition affects each one of us very differently. Though many I have met are very comfortable with their Asperger's Syndrome diagnosis and, like myself, may consider their condition as being part of who they are, there are others I have met who are so proud of the label that they even attach themselves to it and some who, sadly, are either sensitive about it or aren't generally very comfortable with it.

One person diagnosed with Asperger's Syndrome who attended one of my talks said that he was 'shocked' to hear me say that I wouldn't accept a cure for Asperger's Syndrome if one ever became available. When I give a talk about Asperger's Syndrome, as is the case with any other Asperger's Syndrome speaker, it is just one individual's perspective. When saying that I wouldn't accept a cure for Asperger's Syndrome, I am not trying to influence or 'condition' others into thinking that if you are diagnosed with Asperger's Syndrome you shouldn't accept a cure for your condition or encourage professionals not to ever think about developing a cure for Asperger's Syndrome, as it is a personal viewpoint. Even though I wouldn't personally accept a cure for Asperger's Syndrome, I wouldn't deny it to those who would accept it.

Stereotypes about Asperger's Syndrome still often suggest that people diagnosed with the condition can hold very narrow views, and experience difficulty being able to see beyond this. Though this is partly true, it is not to say that it concerns all people with Asperger's Syndrome. Some of the most open and tolerant people I have ever met are diagnosed with Asperger's Syndrome. According to Ajahn Sumedho (2004), a monk based at Amaravati Monastery near Hemel Hempstead in the UK, we are all a product of our 'cultural conditioning', in terms of different values we are brought up with. To go beyond it can take a determined effort, but through development of effective tolerance, one can become 'awakened' rather than 'conditioned'.

How we are conditioned culturally often influences our ways of perceiving and interpreting different values, viewpoints, traditions, etc. To many people with Asperger's Syndrome, such conventions that culturally condition us can be invisible as they are unwritten. In this sense, being blind to such conventions can have an advantage in the sense that because one can't see it, one isn't likely to become conditioned in such a way that it subjects one to biases. In this sense, people diagnosed with Asperger's Syndrome are able to develop tolerance through different eyes, and with mindfulness, can apply it effectively in terms of developing social skills. However, being blind to cultural conditioning can also have disadvantages in the sense that a person with Asperger's Syndrome can't see the unwritten rules as to why others may behave or act in a particular way in a given situation, which can be mistaken for ignorance.

Many people diagnosed with Asperger's Syndrome appear more comfortable socialising with others diagnosed with the condition, feeling that they are more likely to understand them, especially if they feel they have been socially excluded elsewhere. As a person with Asperger's Syndrome, I have often felt this way. At first this may sound socially restrictive through not interacting socially beyond the Asperger community, but as we have seen, individuals with the condition vary dramatically, so within the Asperger community, one who has recently been diagnosed with Asperger's Syndrome when first visiting a social group or joining an autism e-mailing list will more than likely meet many different Asperger personalities.

As well as meeting other, different, individuals diagnosed with Asperger's Syndrome, something that I have also benefited from, and I feel that many others diagnosed with Asperger's Syndrome can gain much insight from, is a balance of interaction with those with Asperger's Syndrome and those not on the autistic spectrum. Social channels I have include networking at work through activities, including playing football, going to gigs and sometimes when I go travelling I am part of a tour group with other travellers.

For me, having different social outlets helps with developing flexibility of my social skills. In different environments, topics of conversation are very different, which gives me awareness as a person with Asperger's Syndrome as to where particular social behaviours are acceptable as well as where they are not appropriate. Having a wide range of interests has also been of help to me in terms of fitting in socially in different environments, but even when one does have such an extensive knowledge of different subjects, mindfulness is needed to know where certain conversation topics are appropriate as well as where to avoid inappropriate social gestures. Being able to relate well to others through different channels not only aids my own tolerance towards others, but others become very accepting of me, even if I sometimes still appear slightly different.

Some people diagnosed with Asperger's Syndrome who do have an extensive range of general knowledge on a variety of topics may also have a tendency to go off on a tangent. As I discussed in Chapter 4, I have had this tendency, but with the discipline of attention, I am able to listen effectively in social situations, and when I am speaking, I am able to recognise when others want to respond without going off on a tangent. In social situations, I often feel much more awakened in this sense.

It is understandable that some people diagnosed with Asperger's Syndrome may not be too eager to develop friendships with people beyond the autistic spectrum, particularly if they feel they have been let down or ill-treated in their recent past. However, openness towards people who are not on the autistic spectrum in terms of interaction can have great rewards in terms of social skills development for a person with Asperger's Syndrome, and a person who isn't on the autistic spectrum who socialises with people with Asperger's Syndrome can develop a tolerance and understanding of Asperger's Syndrome.

Though as an advocate for Asperger's Syndrome I believe that the best way for those who don't have Asperger's Syndrome to understand the condition is to find out from people who have an Asperger's Syndrome diagnosis, to gain a richer understanding of Asperger's Syndrome, it helps to meet with and know a wide range of individuals on the spectrum. Self-advocacy among people diagnosed with Asperger's Syndrome is currently very strong, with there being an extensive range of literature available in the form of autobiographies and self-help books, much more so than there was when I was diagnosed back in 1998, as well as there being many individuals diagnosed with Asperger's Syndrome who take part in public speaking. Just reading an autobiography or listening to a talk by a speaker with Asperger's Syndrome isn't often enough to gain a true understanding of the condition, as it is just one individual's perspective and experiences, and just because such perspectives are given by one individual diagnosed with Asperger's Syndrome, it doesn't mean that the next person diagnosed with Asperger's Syndrome will provide an identical account, written or spoken.

Like those who aren't on the autistic spectrum, people diagnosed with Asperger's Syndrome are found in different races/ethnicities, have different sexual preferences and practise different beliefs. Due to such differences there are likely to be differences of opinion among people diagnosed with Asperger's Syndrome, as much as there are between them and those not on the autistic spectrum. The second hindrance, ill-will, can affect the state of mind of a person with Asperger's Syndrome, particularly a person with Asperger's Syndrome who becomes part of an extremist religion, political organisation or cult that they abide by, to the extent that they try to coerce others into thinking in such ways. Without tolerance, they will develop ill-will, often without realising it or being aware of its consequences, for both those that they are harming and themselves. Doing such harm to others does harm to oneself.

Having previously been at fault for holding onto extremist views, something that I have found that has helped me to avoid attachment is to sample different cultural experiences. After believing in the ideals of Marxism when a university student, seeing how capitalism helped to shape modern American society by allowing creativity and innovation to develop opened me up to accepting ideals that I had previously thought 'evil'. When a university student, I was also a strong anti-monarchist, but seeing what the concept of monarchy meant to the Thais when visiting Thailand made me realise how what some may not be entirely keen on means so much to others.

For me, experience of different cultures has been a good way to develop an attitude of tolerance to other beliefs and ideas that I have known myself to dislike, and sometimes such insight gained through tolerance can open up new friends and interests. Some people with Asperger's Syndrome I have met, and myself to some extent, have developed good friendships with others who have been victim to social prejudice, including ethnic minorities, the gay community, those with mental health difficulties, etc. As many people diagnosed with Asperger's Syndrome feel they may have experienced similar discrimination, they may be more likely to see others as they actually are, rather than how cultural conditioning may see them.

There are some things though that are very difficult for a person with Asperger's Syndrome to tolerate, especially if they have previously been affected by them in their past, such as bullying and facing other such threats and intimidation, both mental and physical. What I have learned though, partly through the practice of loving-kindness meditation (Mettā), is that responding to such ills through holding onto hatred is only giving bullies power, when they see you as vulnerable.

It is known that many adults with Asperger's Syndrome still suffer from the effects of bullying they experienced in the schoolyard, and some have even been treated with similar therapies to those used to treat Vietnam war veterans. Practice of Mettā encourages one to extend their range of benevolence to even those that one finds they may have disliked or even found despicable, so that one finds compassion. Where I have found compassion in relation to the bullying that I suffered during my school days is through understanding that those who bullied me in the schoolyard perhaps didn't know any better, and it could be that now they are older, wherever they are, they perhaps feel a little guilty, like some of my former university colleagues said they felt after they found out I had been diagnosed with Asperger's Syndrome.

How to develop effective tolerance

To be tolerant of others, one doesn't have to like or agree with everything that others support and enjoy, as tolerance can also be associated with naivety. Tolerance is the acceptance of willingness to allow others to be different in their views and actions. For a person diagnosed with Asperger's Syndrome to develop such an effective tolerance, some suggestions include:

- Though it is inevitable you may come across those who differ from you in terms of views and actions, it may help to avoid disliking or hating, which enables you to accept those whose differences you may not be comfortable with.

- Where possible, try to avoid showing anger in response to another who supports a view you feel discriminates against you, as this can make you appear insecure, which they will use to their advantage.

- If the actions of another hurt you mentally or physically, avoid responding in the same way unless you need to defend yourself, as this is only taking you to their level.

Effective tolerance of others can also help you achieve acceptance socially as a person with Asperger's Syndrome as well as opening you up to understanding why others are different:

- To understand why others are different, it may help to find out why others are the way they are, which may be courtesy of their background, upbringing, etc.

- Varied social experiences can also be effective in terms of extending your openness. This can be achieved by observing or even taking part in activities that you may not agree with, for instance if you feel your political views are very left-wing, to gain an opposite view, it may help to experience an environment where views are right-wing. Similarly, if you practise Buddhism, it may help to observe services in other beliefs – Christianity, Islam, etc.

- Look at how your own views and experiences interrelate where possible to those you have experienced differences with. For instance, someone who has experienced similar issues, including depression or low self-esteem, may have a different approach to dealing with or managing them which may help reinforce your understanding of why others do things differently.

How to effectively tolerate people with Asperger's Syndrome

People who are not on the autistic spectrum are just as vulnerable to difficulties that many people with Asperger's Syndrome have experienced, including social isolation, low self-esteem, depression. Opening up to people diagnosed with Asperger's Syndrome can provide insight relating to such suffering, and also develop a deeper understanding of the condition:

- All individuals diagnosed with Asperger's Syndrome are different. To understand this it may help to meet different individuals with Asperger's Syndrome or read different accounts written by people with Asperger's Syndrome.

- As all individuals with Asperger's Syndrome are different, their social perceptions are very different. If a person with Asperger's Syndrome appears awkward or vulnerable socially, try to avoid 'broadcasting' it to others, as this can make them feel that they are not being accepted.

- When trying to include a person with Asperger's Syndrome in a social situation, where possible encourage the person with Asperger's Syndrome to adapt their social characteristics to the situation, rather than encourage them to be someone they're not or 'pretend to be normal' as this distances themselves and others from knowing who they are.

CHAPTER 10

Measuring Success and Goal-setting

How to measure success realistically and achieve without distancing ourselves from truth

As well as having influence on our own personal views and how we treat others, one's cultural conditioning can also influence what we see as success. For an individual with Asperger's Syndrome though, their ways of measuring success and personal happiness are not often conventional. One of the most important things I feel I have learned since my diagnosis is not to live up to anybody's expectations but my own, and to ensure avoidance of extreme disappointment where possible, by keeping my hopes and expectations realistic.

Being brought up in a largely secular Western environment, images often projected of success include being a high achiever academically, being successful in a career, being a high-earner, owning and running your own business or service, owning a property or a few properties, owning a car and being happily married with a family. Such 'success stories' are often put across in promotional literature, including career guidance pamphlets, university/college prospectuses as well as in sections of newspapers and magazines.

Such images of success though are often very superficial, as they are just one person's or a small group's own versions of what they perceive as a success, or what the organisation pro-filing them sees as success. Not everybody can replicate such images of success, and perhaps more so, not everybody may feel comfortable with such experiences of success. Within Buddhist values, the ethos is on happiness and, above all, contentment rather than 'success'. This ethos is particularly visible in the Kingdom of Bhutan, where the preferred measurement of the nation's success is Gross Domestic Happiness rather than the conventional Gross Domestic Product.

Though success can give one a sense of achievement, when it is projected in such a way, what one is often oblivious to at such moments of success is that it is impermanent, rarely lasting. One can acquire a property or achieve a high turnover if running a business, but it may not have long-term value. In a few years time, a property one has acquired may not be suitable any more, or a business's turnover may drop. In relation to this, the Dhammapāda suggests, very truthfully, that when one dies, material possessions are no longer of use to us.

Though there are some individuals with Asperger's Syndrome I have met who have their own effective ways of measuring and managing success and personal happiness, there are many others I have met who experience low self-esteem and even depression through not being able to meet personal expec-tations of themselves or not being able to measure up to their contemporaries. As I mentioned in Chapter 3, I have experi-enced such disappointments in my own life.

A potential source of one setting idealistic hopes and expectations of themselves can possibly relate to unhappiness and frustration in their upbringing. For instance if one has been a victim of bullying during their school life, to compensate for the social isolation they have experienced, they may create an 'invisible friend' or 'imaginary world' where they can retreat to if they feel they are not accepted in their immediate world

(Attwood 1997). This concept can then extend to feeling that one almost deserves to have a better future than others because of what one has previously suffered.

One of my ambitions when coming out of school was to be the next John Motson (respected BBC football commentator). This didn't just relate to my interest in watching football, but it was also connected to the unhappiness and general non-acceptance I felt during my school days. Feeling so angry with what I had had to put up with in the schoolyard, I wanted to 'better myself' and work in a field where I may be accepted and respected for something that I may like doing, and for those who made my life difficult in the schoolyard I wanted them to experience futures of failure and suffering.

When I look back at the way I was during this time, becoming preoccupied by what I wanted for myself and for many of my contemporaries only distanced me from reality. It wasn't until I was older that I found out through experience that top football commentating jobs are few and far between, not to mention competition for them is intense. As my focus was so narrow on what I ideally wanted to do with my life, I forgot about what else I may be doing, such as working in an office or call-centre.

It is well documented that some individuals diagnosed with Asperger's Syndrome have special interests in certain subjects and in some cases have specialist skills or expertise. There are also success stories about people diagnosed with Asperger's Syndrome, in particular Dr Temple Grandin, who have been able to make a career out of their specialist interest or skill, in Grandin's case cattle-chute design. Such individuals are known as 'autistic savants'. Though autistic savants deserve admiration for their achievements, in a more indirect sense, they can also create false hopes in individuals with Asperger's Syndrome, as well as in others who may think that 'my daughter can be just like Temple Grandin'.

Such false hopes can turn into idealistic and often unreal aspirations. The more such false aspirations build up in a person with Asperger's Syndrome, the more the mind creates images of what they ultimately aim to reach to the extent that it can go beyond reality. I have met others with Asperger's Syndrome who went through a similar phase of feeling that they automatically deserve their ideal job and a good lifestyle for what they have suffered. This ultimately brings disappointment when one realises that they have set standards too high or expected too much.

The I-ness or self-ness of a person mentally outlining what they feel they deserve or setting their own unrealistic aspirations can not only distance one from truth, but can also lead towards further suffering in the form of low self-esteem and possibly depression. Such self-ness can ultimately lead to one becoming concerned with how they measure up to others, creating irrelevant distractions, to the extent that one may avoid social situations where they may feel inferior to others around them, or feel distanced from others in that they can't live up to their conditioned standards. Distancing oneself from others they feel inferior to only gives others power, and exposes one to the hindrance of ill-will, where one dislikes others through envy.

The teachings of the Buddha identify five component parts, or 'Khandas', of sensory perception that contribute to such irrational distractions. The Five Khandas are as follows:

1. **rūpa** – physical phenomena

2. **vedanā** – feelings of pleasure, pain or indifference

3. **saññā** – concepts, labels and allusions

4. **saṅkhāra** – mental fashioning, formations and processes

5. **viññāṇa** – sensory consciousness.

The Khandas make up personality, determining different mind states a person experiences from happiness through to unhappiness and indifference as well as calmness, anger, fear and excitement. According to Phra Ajaan Mun Bhuridatta Mahatera (1870–1949), a highly respected Thai monk, the tricks of sañña make the mind spin, going wrong through trusting its saññas (2000). Through practice of Vipassana meditation, I have found it helpful to recognise the Khandas, so that I can see why things are the way they are in relation to me in accordance with my surroundings. All of us have our visions for the way we want things to be for ourselves, and people diagnosed with Asperger's Syndrome are no different, particularly if they find changes in their own circumstances or in society generally difficult. Through recognising the Khandas, I have found that the more one wants things to be the way they want them to be, the more this can expose one to dukkha.

When one becomes over-immersed in such mental states, one can lose mindfulness. I used to experience such feeling when a university student, often feeling inferior to career-minded high-flyers, but now when I reflect on this, I realise that it was all largely just an irrational fear. What can cause even lower self-esteem than a person with Asperger's Syndrome comparing him- or herself to others is when people who are not on the autistic spectrum compare him or her with others.

The low self-esteem and inferiority one can experience when measuring up to others has taught me that, as a person with Asperger's Syndrome, the most effective way for me to measure success is in accordance with what I feel my capabilities are. To do this effectively, I find that being aware of my strengths and weaknesses helps as well as what I have come through to achieve. For me to have been accepted into university in the first place after needing extra help with certain subjects, particularly maths, when at school was an achievement, and eventually graduating from university despite what I went through was also an achievement.

More beneficial than measuring success itself though, I find is measuring personal happiness and contentment. Although achieving success itself gives one a sense of achievement that enables self-confidence, its nature is often impermanent. One may have success in securing a high-profile job, but then may experience suffering from the stress and pressure that such a position involves. What was initially a frustration for me was having to make do with positions that only required GCSEs despite being university educated. But in different environments where I have worked, I have come across people who always seem to be wanting a promotion and in some cases envy those who have higher-grade positions than they do, and even when one achieves a promotion and pay rise they want another one almost immediately. People from all walks of life experience frustration: rich and poor, successful and not so successful as well as people diagnosed with Asperger's Syndrome and related conditions. An individual on a low to middle income may experience frustration in perhaps wanting to do and achieve more than just 'getting by', whereas at another extreme, a stockbroker may experience frustration when their stocks/shares lose value after a period of prosperity. Such is the impermanence of success that if one doesn't realise it, they will never be happy and content.

For me, the most important factor in me being happy in a job is being valued and well liked by my colleagues and having the ability to make a positive difference to the lives of others. Even if I am providing general admin support, including typing letters, filing, sorting post, I still take heart from being a link in a process that enables people to obtain access to information and documents that make the difference in terms of what support, benefits, etc. they are entitled to. Just being in any kind of full-time stable employment though is an achievement for me after what I have experienced in terms of so many disappointments and frustrations with failed applications.

Another measurement of personal happiness for me has been in terms of how I feel I have progressed socially since being diagnosed. After years of social isolation and general difficulty in maintaining long-term friendships, to have developed the network of friends that I now have, including those diagnosed with Asperger's Syndrome and others not on the autistic spectrum, has given me a strong sense of happiness through insight. I find it more beneficial and, personally, more stable to measure personal happiness in terms of long-term well-being rather than short bursts of material success.

By saying that one setting goals and ambitions can lead to frustration, I am not trying to suggest that one shouldn't set personal goals, not least because the Eightfold Path, or 'The Middle Way', in the teachings of the Buddha outlines goals that its followers hope to attain, including happiness, contentment and ultimately Nirvana, a state of everlasting peace beyond living. Goal-setting, if done realistically while applying the patience to see it through can also be a motivating force, thus avoiding being affected by the hindrance of sloth and torpor.

The goals set out along The Middle Way can be more difficult for many to achieve than material goals that arise out of the hindrance of sense desire. My ultimate personal goal is that of continual happiness and contentment. To some, this may sound like lacking in ambition, but even basic personal happiness and general contentment needs to be maintained. To maintain such happiness, I try to look at everything I do each day in a positive way, looking at positive benefits that my actions have wherever possible, even looking at positive actions from any mistakes I unintentionally make or from any difficulties I experience.

When one is trying to reach a goal, whether it is trying to achieve something academically, such as achieving high grades or just obtaining a qualification, or professionally, such as obtaining employment or gaining promotion, or trying to achieve general contentment, one will inevitably experience difficult phases where the hindrance of doubt may stand in one's way. When going through a difficult period during completing a course, project, task, etc., there may be periods where one has to stop to review their progress and concentrate their energy and focus, so that they can see the next stage in a more clear and skilled way, enabling them to continue towards completion.

An analogy that I like to use when describing coping with this is mountains and base camps. Climbing a mountain is a challenge where one has to overcome many difficult frontiers and mental hindrances, like I found with completing university. After having struggled climbing over steep rocks and negotiating slippery paths or completing essays and sitting exams and perhaps not feeling any gain, one may begin to question themselves as to what it is all worth in the end. I often felt this way when an undergraduate university student midway through my degree, where I had begun to doubt what the use of continuing studying would be, and had thought of changing direction in life rather than staying on to complete my degree. But the lay-off that I had from study enabled me in the end to see the value of staying on and obtaining the qualification, as completion could enable me to pursue further study, whereas if I had dropped out, I would only have had half a degree, which I had put some work into, but would have had nothing to show for it.

As many people with Asperger's Syndrome feel they face an uphill battle to make progress in terms of their education or in obtaining employment and working their way up, goal-setting to reach these and other related targets can be a strong motivating force. But to avoid vulnerability to low-self-esteem, it helps one to focus their goal so that it is set realistically. Though concentration and patience are required to focus and see through to attaining goals, mindfulness can also help one to be aware of any potential difficult phases one may have to go through on the way towards attaining a goal as well as help prepare one for how to handle such situations appropriately.

How to measure success effectively

All individuals with Asperger's Syndrome have their own different ways of measuring success. Such ways could be related to their personal values, or in some cases special interests. Here are some suggestions for maintaining self-esteem alongside success:

- To gain a sense of personal achievement, it may be of help to review your progress (academically, professionally, etc.) in accordance with your own capabilities.

- Try to avoid measuring your progress with others, as this can lead to irrelevant distractions that can cause hindrances to your self-esteem.

- Not everyone can attain the same achievements as one another, and rarely can one achieve standards expected or hoped for by others. To avoid low self-esteem, it may help one to live up to their own expectations, rather than those of others.

How to encourage a person with Asperger's Syndrome to develop a sense of personal achievement and self-esteem

The way people with Asperger's Syndrome measure success and happiness in terms of achievement and personal values is, again, often very different to the way people who are not on the autistic spectrum may perceive success, as well as often being different to 'conditioned' success:

- To encourage self-esteem in terms of a person with Asperger's Syndrome measuring their progress and success, it may help to focus on their positive aspects, as this will help the person understand what they may be capable of.

- Try to avoid judging a person with Asperger's Syndrome by your own standards or 'conventional' standards, as this can make the person feel inadequate or subject to irrelevant distractions.

- A person with Asperger's Syndrome may have personal values which are not only very different from your own, but sometimes very unconventional. Where possible, avoid judging a person with Asperger's Syndrome by your own values, as this can again subject the person to inadequacy, not measuring up to others.

How to set goals realistically

It helps to have personal goals, as they can be a strong source of motivation and can help with development of mindfulness, if one sets about achieving them accordingly. However, goal-setting can also be a source of frustration, if one sets their standards too high or unrealistically. Here are some suggestions on how to set and achieve goals realistically and accordingly:

- Before identifying your personal goal, it may help you to assess in accordance with your strengths and weaknesses and general capabilities what you feel you can realistically achieve.

- Try to avoid setting your personal standards too high. Though high standards can be a motivational force, they can only go so high. The mind can become subject to overload and never satisfied, become subject to fear of failure.

- To reach goals, it often takes a lot of patience, especially if one struggles along the way and begins to doubt about whether they will achieve their goal. If this occurs, it may help to take a break and recollect one's energies and focus before continuing the path.

How to support a person with Asperger's Syndrome in setting and achieving goals

Often, a person with Asperger's Syndrome may benefit from positive encouragement in terms of achieving goals, especially if and when facing difficulties along the way. Self-confidence is an important factor in working towards and achieving goals. If you support a person with Asperger's Syndrome as a parent, carer, sibling, etc. it may help to:

- Try not to expect anything 'special' or 'dramatic' from the individual straight away, as this can put pressure on the person with Asperger's Syndrome. To do this effectively, try to put yourself in their shoes by remembering how it may have been for you as a beginner in different situations (e.g. starting a new job, learning a new task).

- If the person experiences any difficulties in terms of working towards their goal, try to avoid reacting angrily, as this can make the person feel they have failed.

- To encourage not giving up, it may help to encourage the person to recollect their energies and focus by focusing on what they have already achieved along the way, and perhaps work out in cooperation with the person how this can be transferred to the next stage of the process.

CHAPTER 11

Facing and Coping
with Suffering

How to manage feelings of suffering (dukkhā)
through reflection

⸺⸺

The previous chapter discussed how suffering (dukkhā in Pāli) can arise through one not being happy with the way things are, often because we want things to be a particular way. Individuals with Asperger's Syndrome may want things to be a particular way for various reasons, which could be related to a preference for order and structure, or in some cases could be related to obsessive-compulsive tendencies. Being diagnosed with Asperger's Syndrome can be a huge relief when one finds a reason for why they are the way they are, but such feeling is impermanent. As Asperger's Syndrome is a lifelong condition, one diagnosed with the condition is likely to experience highs and lows associated with it beyond diagnosis. This chapter looks at how one can manage dukkhā at the point of diagnosis and beyond so that it doesn't take control of the mind, and also how one can learn from coping with suffering.

As well as an unhappiness with the way the present is, people diagnosed with Asperger's Syndrome, especially those diagnosed late in life, can experience dukkhā in the form of frustration and regret for past actions and experiences related to undiagnosed Asperger's Syndrome in terms of how much better things could have perhaps been if diagnosed earlier. For others with the condition, such feeling may also be related to 'I should have things better'. The First Noble Truth in the Buddha's teachings suggests dukkhā is conditioned by such cravings and clinging desires, but if these can be undermined, dukkhā can be curtailed. In the media, people diagnosed with Asperger's Syndrome, including myself, are often referred to as 'suffering' from Asperger's Syndrome. For me though, what I felt was suffering was remaining undiagnosed until I was 20 years old, often knowing I was different but not knowing of any reason as to why. When I was first diagnosed, I felt for the first time I could assess myself effectively in terms of strengths and weaknesses and how I could adapt these to my surroundings and in relation to others in terms of social integration. As well as being able to adapt the way I was courtesy of my diagnosis to the present and future, for the first time I also became much clearer about the actions and experiences of my past.

Many adults with Asperger's Syndrome that I have met, especially those diagnosed late in life, including people over 60 years old, when diagnosed, have often felt similar feelings in terms of how they were able to review their life appropriately for the first time, in terms of issues such as difficulty with social situations, failed relationships, difficulty holding down a job, etc. Being able to reflect on one's past in such a way, knowing there was a reason for why one did things the way they did in their past can help one overcome the hindrance of restlessness and remorse, and also feelings of guilt.

In Chapter 9 I mentioned that I wouldn't deny a cure of Asperger's Syndrome to anyone diagnosed with the condition if ever one became available if they so wanted it. Though myself and many other people diagnosed with Asperger's Syndrome are generally very comfortable with their diagnosis and appear to cope effectively, I have also come across some individuals who feel vulnerable with an Asperger's Syndrome diagnosis.

Personally though, I feel from what I have learned that being aware of how Asperger's Syndrome affects a person can enable one to put their diagnosis into the context of different surroundings and situations they may find themselves in. In turn, this can help explain different mind states, positive and negative, that one may be subject to in different situations.

Like many other people diagnosed with Asperger's Syndrome, I experienced at times extreme levels of ups and downs. Writing my autobiography (Mitchell 2005), when I look back now, was almost like an extended Vipassanā practice in the sense that writing it involved gathering and reviewing some of the most difficult periods in my life. Something that I found when thinking about emotionally difficult periods, such as the depression I experienced while at university, was that the extent to which one can be hurt emotionally when remembering such periods can cloud out happier times. But through balancing difficult periods with happier times, I found that such suffering is impermanent, and that to some extent it helps to remember how one may have felt through difficult times, including what one may have learned through such experiences, without becoming attached to them to the extent that one finds themselves living with the effects of such times rather than letting them go through moving on. This can also help one relate to others who experience similar difficulties, as well as one's own development of effective coping strategies.

According to Ajahn Sumedho (2004), the way to understand suffering is to open up to it, including recognising its roots and effects. HH The Dalai Lama, with Dr Howard C. Cutler, in the international best-selling *The Art of Happiness* (1998) similarly suggest that perhaps the best way to understand and cope with suffering is to observe the roots of suffering and tolerate them before slowly removing them. To both recognise and acknowledge roots of suffering can also open up one to learn from the experience and then move on. After all, suffering, like the other extreme, joy, is an impermanent phenomenon.

For me, through learning from my past, when writing my autobiography (Mitchell 2005), and Vipassanā practice, I have found that it helps, as a person diagnosed with Asperger's Syndrome relatively late in life, to contemplate my past rather than dwell on it or attach myself to it. Not long after I had been diagnosed, when going over my past, I felt much frustration in terms of how I felt unable to make decisions effectively concerning my future in relation to my strengths and weaknesses, and as a result I experienced difficulties with transitions from school to university, from university to work and to independent living generally. I was unhappy with what had happened, because now that I knew who I was, I wanted things to have happened in a particular way so that much of what I felt I suffered could have been avoided.

For a while I pretended that the first 20 years of my life didn't exist, that I had been someone who didn't exist. Though I needed to make a new start in terms of 're-inventing' myself in accordance with what I now knew about who I was, more recently, observance of immediate experience through Vipassanā practice in reflecting rather than dwelling on my past has helped me understand what has caused much of my personal suffering.

One of the major factors that has caused much suffering for me, and has caused much suffering for many other adults with Asperger's Syndrome diagnosed relatively late in life, in particular my friend Garry Burge, whose life in many ways parallels my own in terms of being diagnosed quite late in life (Garry was 26 years old when diagnosed), is social isolation. When one is experiencing much personal unsatisfaction, the mind often questions 'why me and not anybody else?' and much anxiety begins to build up. It is often easy for one to think during such periods that, while one is suffering, others have it so much better, and to be oblivious to the fact that, however happy or successful other people around you may appear, they also experience dukkhā in their own ways, albeit a form of dukkhā that many adults with Asperger's Syndrome perhaps can't relate to.

I didn't realise it at the time, but there were other people around my age who were going through what I had been through, in terms of suffering from social isolation and beginning to wonder if they may have Asperger's Syndrome. Though Garry was the first other adult diagnosed with Asperger's Syndrome in similar circumstances to my own that I got to know well, through subscription to Autuniv-1 (an autism e-mailing list), I got to know others in similar situations, all of who had very different ways of dealing with frustration, which has provided me with valuable insight in terms of dealing with my own suffering. My own ways of dealing with suffering, I feel, have had effects on others in terms of finding meaning in suffering.

As well as understanding the roots of suffering, HH The Dalai Lama (1998) also encourages one to find meaning in dukkhā, in particular to learn from what one may experience in dukkhā, and in some cases, what dukkhā can enable in terms of insight and developing ways to cope effectively with its effects. For me, the meaning that I found in dukkhā that I experienced prior to diagnosis enabled me to find who I am, with the diagnosis providing the truth. Like me, many other people with Asperger's Syndrome appear to have come into contact with others diagnosed with the condition courtesy of shared experiences of suffering and frustration that they can relate to and can provide one another with valuable insight.

When studying for my MA (Hons), I found that the Asperger population is very thinly spread throughout the world, rarely appearing 'clustered' together in certain areas, but the availability of access to the internet had enabled the Asperger population to 'discover itself', through autism e-mailing lists such as Autuniv-1 (Dekker 1998). But even before accessing the internet to come into contact with other people diagnosed with the condition, a factor that has brought the Asperger community together has been dukkhā.

The suffering through social isolation that a person with Asperger's Syndrome experiences, however difficult and unpleasant, can lead one to seek out others with the condition through joining autism e-mailing lists or looking for potential pen-friends with the condition. This is where, as a person with Asperger's Syndrome, I feel I have found a meaning in my own suffering, as if I hadn't had such experiences, I wouldn't have known friends like Garry, Tara and others I have since met, and thus wouldn't know about me what I now know. The ability of dukkhā to bring together the Asperger community to provide one another with insight, I feel, can, despite what those who have experienced it have been through, be the meaning of suffering for many people with Asperger's Syndrome.

As well as social isolation, people diagnosed with Asperger's Syndrome can experience many other forms of dukkhā, which can also be influenced by factors such as their age:

- Children and teenagers diagnosed with Asperger's Syndrome may experience dukkhā through not being understood and often being manipulated by their peers.

- Teenagers and young adults diagnosed with Asperger's Syndrome may experience dukkhā through social inadequacy and other social phobias, such as a fear of getting a 'raw deal' or being 'ripped off'.

- Young to middle-aged adults diagnosed with Asperger's Syndrome may experience dukkhā through feeling unable to access what others their age appear to have no problems accessing (e.g. good job market, relationships, property ladder).

- Some older people diagnosed with Asperger's Syndrome, especially those diagnosed late in life, may feel full of regret for past actions in relation to not knowing any reason behind them, and may feel that diagnosis is too late to have any benefit.

Often, what many people diagnosed with Asperger's Syndrome want out of life is what many others want, and such want is often a root of suffering. However, Ajahn Sumedho (2004) suggests that suffering should be 'welcomed', because it is impermanent, it doesn't last. The sources that bring about suffering, including frustration, disappointment, inadequacy and jealousy, are as impermanent as the sources of joy. But as people with Asperger's Syndrome can become strongly fixated in a particular mind-set, negative or positive, it can be easy to become unmindful of the changing circumstances that contribute to their mind-set.

Like other people with Asperger's Syndrome, I have experienced feelings of inadequacy and inferiority in various social situations, sometimes even in Asperger social groups. Where I have seen people with Asperger's Syndrome experience dukkhā in situations around other people with Asperger's Syndrome is where a person with Asperger's Syndrome is successful in a particular field, particularly in science and mathematics-related fields, and another person with Asperger's Syndrome, whose strengths are in arts-related fields, feels that it is harder for them to find a career. When Garry visited me in England in 2001, we went to meet Mark, a university student with Asperger's Syndrome in the process of completing a PhD in Particle Physics. The first thing Garry noted when we met Mark was that it appeared much easier for people with Asperger's Syndrome whose strengths/interests were in a maths or science-related field to make a success of their lives.

Different topics of conversation in social situations about how successful different people are, in terms of their social and professional progress, include gaining promotion to management/supervisory positions, salary increases, or elsewhere getting married and raising a family successfully. A person diagnosed with Asperger's Syndrome might not often be able to relate to these. However, the person with Asperger's Syndrome, often unable to read between the lines of social interaction, may not also realise that, however successful others may appear to be, they may also experience their own dukkhā. People in management/supervisory positions may experience much stress associated with their roles while someone who is successful in business may feel insecure about losing their wealth or facing competition. In this sense, as well as bringing together the Asperger community itself, dukkhā can also bring together people with Asperger's Syndrome and people who are not on the autistic spectrum.

An awareness of different circumstances, through reflection and acknowledgement rather than ignorance of them, can be a surprisingly good way of coping with dukkhā for a person with Asperger's Syndrome, enabling one to retain confidence in social situations, rather than feeling distanced from them. If one understands that dukkhā can unite both people with Asperger's Syndrome and people not on the autistic spectrum, it is possible that one is less likely to be subject to feelings, including jealousy, inadequacy and inferiority, that create dukkhā.

Vipassanā practice has enabled me to both welcome dukkhā and find meaning in it, and, perhaps most importantly, to recognise it. Personally I feel that the more a person diagnosed with Asperger's Syndrome can become aware of dukkhā, not just in terms of how it affects oneself, but also how it affects others, the more enlightened the person becomes. Here are some suggestions on how to find awareness of and manage dukkhā from different sources and as experienced in different situations:

How to manage feelings of dukkhā effectively

As Asperger's Syndrome is a lifelong condition, sadly the 'ups' and downs' associated with it are often likely to be experienced by one diagnosed with the condition through life, including not being happy with the way one's surroundings are, wanting them to be different. If one can notice impermanence within ups and downs through being able to reflect on surroundings rather than ignoring them, it may help one see things in context more clearly:

- If you experience a period of difficulty or low self-esteem, remember that such periods aren't likely to last, and that with the right effort and patience needed to think positive thought combined with awareness, you may be able to find a way out without resorting to anger.

- At the other extreme, you may experience a period where you are happy and joyful, but, like dukkhā such a state is also impermanent. It may help to try to avoid excessive excitement so that if and when your circumstances change, you may be less likely to experience depression and low self-esteem and be able to manage circumstances in a more skilled, mindful way.

- Try to recognise such impermanence as a 'quality' in relation to your surroundings, including things and other people you may be reliant on – recognise what could potentially happen (e.g. your car could fail, you could be laid off work). This way, you may recognise potential sources of dukkhā, enabling effective preparation for when they arise, and be able to let go of suffering effectively without resorting to anger.

Social situations

Many people with Asperger's Syndrome feel that, in social situations, they often have to 'pretend to be normal' or pretend to be 'something they're not'. As a person with Asperger's Syndrome, you may have experienced feelings of vulnerability or inadequacy in social situations, including working environments, parties, casual social gatherings and other social events such as conferences, weddings, celebrations. This could be to do with feeling 'out of place' with or inferior to others. To curtail such feelings, it may help to be aware that:

- All individuals, both those diagnosed with Asperger's Syndrome and those not on the autistic spectrum, are just as subject to dukkhā as one another. Looking at things from other perspectives, including from the perspectives of those around you, may help you become more aware as to how dukkhā affects others differently, enabling tactfulness.

- If, in social situations, you find yourself feeling inferior to others when the subject of discussion is how well one is doing or how successful they are in terms of their position, what they own, etc., it may help to be aware that it is one person's edited version of events, so they are likely to cover up the parts they don't like to admit to. But to avoid showing feelings of envy, it may be helpful generally to be happy for others.

- Where possible, try to adapt who you are to the situation rather than feeling you have to pretend to be something you're not. This way, people can get to know who you actually are, which can be good for your self-esteem.

Reflecting on the past

Many people with Asperger's Syndrome, especially those diagnosed late in life, can feel regretful about past actions and
experiences, in the schoolyard, through university, at work, in
relationships (both social and intimate). But if experiencing a
difficult period, an awareness of your past may help you handle
it more effectively:

- If you have experienced a similar period in your past, it
  may help to review how you handled it and came out of
  it previously, as this experience can be used to your advantage in handling the present.

- In this sense, dukkhā can strengthen one mentally and
  also be a tool in developing empathy and sensitivity, including how to exercise these qualities effectively.

- It may also help to look at your past in a reflective way,
  especially if you have recently been diagnosed with
  Asperger's Syndrome or suspect you may have it. Reviewing your past actions rather than blaming or re-
  gretting them can help to remove feelings of guilt and
  allow for clearer consideration of present and future
  actions.

Supporting a person with Asperger's Syndrome during difficult periods

Many people with Asperger's Syndrome can experience low
self-esteem due to social inadequacy. Suggestions to help
develop self-esteem in a person with Asperger's Syndrome if
you are a parent, carer, social worker or employer include:

- Try to avoid cynical comments like 'pull yourself together', 'get over it'. These can display a lack of sensitivity towards a person with Asperger's Syndrome,

contributing to low self-esteem and a lack of confidence.

- Avoid accusing a person with Asperger's Syndrome of 'using their diagnosis as an excuse' for their actions, especially if the person has unintentionally upset someone through blindness to unwritten rules of social interaction.

- Where possible, encourage the person with Asperger's Syndrome to look for the positive aspects that come out of everything, including mistakes.

CHAPTER 12

Finding Balance in Mindfulness and Concentration

How to take responsibility for one's own world and recognise the worlds others live within

When I first mentioned to my meditation teacher that I am diagnosed with Asperger's Syndrome, he said that, from what he knew, people with the condition often display quite high levels of concentration, especially relating to ability to focus on a specialist subject. Though being able to concentrate in such a way can be a useful quality to have, if one has obsessive-compulsive tendencies, it can be easy to become lost within such concentration. This is why I find, as a person with Asperger's Syndrome, it helps to balance such concentration with mindfulness, so one can retain awareness of their surroundings and the world they live in generally.

Many textbooks and guidance literature, when describing the conditions of autism and Asperger's Syndrome, often describe people on the autistic spectrum as 'living in their own world'. Though this is largely true, the teachings within Buddhism suggest that *all* individuals live in their own world, a creation of the mind, largely perceiving their surroundings through the perspective of the self. We selectively notice aspects of our surroundings and the wider world around us, noticing according to our likes and dislikes, our pleasures and sufferings, often creating personal biases in terms of how we perceive our surroundings. People with Asperger's Syndrome, however, often pay attention to their surroundings differently. This chapter looks at how awareness gained from Samatha and Vipassanā practice as well as social experience can help one develop the mindfulness needed to take responsibility for one's own world while simultaneously retaining awareness beyond our minds.

When I give training on the subject of Asperger's Syndrome, I like to give audiences an idea of how it may actually feel mentally and physically to be a person diagnosed with the condition. To do this, I often ask them to imagine placing themselves outside their comfort zone, for example, trying to find their way around a country where the first language is one they don't know how to speak, and the body language is different to what they are used to. Initially, when first diagnosed, something that I found very awkward about the condition was how hard it was to understand the workings of the minds of people not on the autistic spectrum. But when I first started speaking publicly about Asperger's Syndrome, and I saw different audiences wanting to understand the condition more, I began to realise that it could be just as hard for them to understand Asperger minds.

Being diagnosed with Asperger's Syndrome, I have often found it difficult to realise how the way I perceive my surroundings in accordance with the way I think doesn't often fit in with the way others might. For example, I still sometimes find certain circumstances hilarious that many others may not. Other people with Asperger's Syndrome I have met often have similar difficulties with awareness of time and place for talking about sensitive issues such as politics and religion, not realising how this can be misinterpreted as unacceptable in certain circumstances. There are some mind qualities, however, that Asperger's Syndrome can enable. In my case, I have often considered myself to be very left-of-brain dominated (the left side of the brain being where knowledge accumulated is stored, with the right side being the part enabling social relationships and awareness) in terms of my memory, concentration and eye for detail. Other people have told me that they 'would love to have a memory like mine', especially if they notice how easy I find it to memorise details of cricket scorecards, film credit lists, and other information, facts and figures.

I have noticed such qualities in many people diagnosed with Asperger's Syndrome, in terms of how they are able to apply themselves effectively to a collection or display relating to a special interest. Many professionals specialising in Asperger's Syndrome are often intrigued at how remarkable artwork by people with Asperger's Syndrome is in terms of its detail. Asperger minds can have strengths, particularly in terms of ability to specialise, through ability to store high volumes of information and the ability to concentrate within a specialist subject or field. Concentration is also a necessary tool for meditation, particularly for noticing and adjusting to different stages during meditation practice, while memory is a necessary tool for chanting in terms of being able to retain different chants recited during practice.

However, such mind strengths associated with Asperger's Syndrome can also cut one diagnosed with the condition off from their surroundings. Such excessive concentration, eye for detail and memory, if over-used, can cause overload and one can lose awareness of their surroundings if they find themselves immersed in an interest, hobby or specialist subject, and can develop narrow perspectives in terms of interpreting their surroundings, seeing the world around them from the perception of their way of thinking. Drawing on special interests I have become immersed in as a person diagnosed with Asperger's Syndrome, I used to try and initiate conversations using different topics such as cricket or politics but didn't always realise that the person I was trying to initiate the conversation with wasn't interested. This is where development of mindfulness can help the individual gain a better understanding of their surroundings, including ability to understand different attitudes of others towards them and avoiding immersion or attachment.

One of the reasons why I first looked into practising meditation was, incidentally, to develop more mind flexibility, as this was an aspect of my mind I had never realised. Though I had often been comfortable with having a strong left-side of brain in terms of recall, where I so often used to experience frustration courtesy of this was an inability to apply the knowledge I could retain to tasks, exams, projects and problem-solving situations. In academic situations, at school and university, I used to experience frustration in terms of doing so much revision but not being able to see how to apply it in exams, while in work situations I have often found it difficult to apply task theory to actual tasks in a working environment. To apply such information and knowledge, one often needs mindfulness to 'see' where the knowledge of a concept or method applies to a particular situation and mind flexibility to see what knowledge is relevant or irrelevant to the situation.

When starting meditation, I told my teacher why I had been interested in pursuing it. When I mentioned Asperger's Syndrome, something that my teacher said that he had heard of in relation to the condition was that those diagnosed with it often have high levels of concentration in terms of becoming fixated in a special interest or obsession. When I told him that this was true and many people with Asperger's Syndrome display such characteristics, something he then mentioned, which encouraged me to persist with meditation, was that one can retain these mind qualities, but with development of mindfulness, can be in control of their surroundings. In this way, development of mindfulness can enable one to be a person with Asperger's Syndrome but simultaneously perceive and interact with their surroundings appropriately.

In Chapter 8, I mentioned how over-reliance upon routine can cause dukkhā if disrupted. With routine, traits and rituals that become associated with it often develop and, in some individuals with Asperger's Syndrome, can become necessary for their comfort, even to the extent where if such traits are disrupted it can cause insecurity. Human beings, both people with Asperger's Syndrome and those not on the autistic spectrum, are creatures of habit and have personal preferences for doing things (e.g. brushing teeth, washing dishes, eating a meal) that are often unique to their own personal world. To have one's own rituals and traits is fine, as long as one doesn't come to depend on them, as this can lead to insecurity and loss of mindfulness.

Being diagnosed with Asperger's Syndrome, I have often found myself over-dependent on traits, routines and rituals that I have developed at different times in my life. Traits and customs that I have become used to over the years include buying the same things in the same shops each week (e.g. same crisps, same candy) to the point where shopkeepers have noticed, so that when they are running out of stock of what I buy on a regular basis, they have kept whatever is left behind the counter expecting me! Elsewhere, I have found myself picking up the same items in shopping baskets, visiting the same supermarket, and checking the same books out of my local library each time!

It is not uncommon for people diagnosed with Asperger's Syndrome to follow such preferential patterns, and this is fine, especially if it makes the individual secure. But where problems can arise is if, for any reason, such patterns have to change. Listening to a talk by Brahmavamso (2003) on obsessions and addictions, I found some strategies he mentioned helpful to avoid over-dependence on traits. Brahmavamso, an English-born monk, based in Western Australia suggests that when humans, being creatures of habit, become over-dependent on such daily traits and routines, they can not only lose mindfulness, but can also become subject to the hindrance of sloth and torpor. Among the ideas for developing mindfulness Brahmavamso suggested in his 2003 talk were to look at different things you do in daily life, such as brushing your teeth. When brushing your teeth, you may have a tendency to start in the same place each time, but the next time you brush your teeth, try starting in a different place.

Since listening to Brahmavamso (2003), I have, where possible, tried to do things in my daily life slightly differently each time. One of these changes that I have made occasionally during daily life is altering my route when driving to work. I have found that if I take the same route each time, I become so used to it that I almost expect the journey to be similar each time. This causes problems when there is an interruption such as if an accident occurs or there is road maintenance taking place, as I have to act quickly to negotiate the situation appropriately. Taking a different route occasionally when driving I find helpful as it helps me understand different roads and see different situations, noticing how such situations occur. This in turn helps me when driving along my 'normal' route to work, as I can notice, through mindfulness, different things each time.

Within meditation practice, I have found it useful to apply such ideas to how I go about it, including occasionally practising at different times during the day. Though most of my practice tends to be done on evenings after coming home from work and having eaten, I have found it helpful to practise during mornings and sometimes around midday over weekends or during days off. Though I have my preferred route through the stages during meditation, occasionally going across a different route reinforces mindfulness, which can be brought effectively into daily life situations.

Doing things differently on occasions can help one notice their surroundings in accordance to the world created by the mind that they live in, including how others who live in very different worlds interpret one's own world, and in terms of being able to notice aspects of one's surroundings that the mind's edited version can often hide. It can often take much practice and effort to develop the mindfulness needed to recognise how one's own world is a creation of the mind, as well as the worlds others live in.

What can so often be difficult for a person with Asperger's Syndrome is being able to recognise how actions they take within their own world affect others and how the actions of others within their worlds affect the world of the person with Asperger's Syndrome. Through development of mindfulness though, one can recognise their own mind-perceived world in accordance with their immediate physical and material surroundings, as well as the worlds that others live in. This can allow for greater responsibility for one's own world and a stronger understanding together with a degree of respect for the worlds of others.

Benefits of mindfulness

Mindfulness is not developed overnight. It can takes months or even years of right effort and concentration to cultivate the mind. But if one is willing to put in the time, potential benefits of mindfulness include:

- Mindfulness can help one assert greater responsibility in relation to their world through awareness, both physical and social.

- It can open one beyond narrow fixations related to Asperger's Syndrome, without taking away special interests or hobbies, but not becoming lost or attached in them.

- Being mindful can help one avoid excessive reliance on conditioned traits/habits.

- Mindfulness can help one to recognise thinking patterns, including the Five Hindrances, that cause problems such as low self-esteem and depression and to let them pass by without 'holding onto them'.

Doing it differently

Though meditation is a tool for developing mindfulness, there are other simpler ways to develop mindfulness through occasionally altering daily routines. Making occasional changes to one's regular pattern for daily living can help one open up to new perspectives, as well as help plan for changes one may have to make due to unforeseen circumstances:

- Look at how you go about daily living, including noticing where you do things more or less the same each day. Work out what you can try doing slightly differently.

- Though you may feel more comfortable with your preferred routes and methods, it may help to occasionally try going about things differently. For example, when brushing your teeth, start in a different place to where you normally start, or take a different route to work, college or university, or when undertaking a journey you take frequently (whether driving, walking or taking public transport).

- Much of how one perceives the world around them can be fed through what we read, see and hear through newspapers/magazines, television and radio. Different programmes/publications within these sources can have their own viewpoints/biases. To gain a different perspective, it may help to occasionally read different publications to what you may normally read or listen and watch different radio/television programmes.

Recognising mindfulness

If you are interested in developing mindfulness as a person with Asperger's Syndrome, it may help to review your progress as you develop. Indications of how to recognise progression in terms of mindfulness include:

- more efficient when studying and learning tasks

- able to apply knowledge and thinking to problem-solving more effectively

- not as subject to narrow fixations or addictions

- aware of hindrances and inconveniences, but not feeling 'pressurised' by them

- able to respond to and perceive different people and circumstances in a non-judgemental way

- general increase in appreciation of living, even when undertaking mediocre tasks (e.g. washing dishes, filling in forms) and feeling less bored or depressed.

CHAPTER 13

Overcoming the Hindrances

How a person with Asperger's Syndrome can overcome difficulties associated with the Five Hindrances through recognition of the Five Spiritual Faculties

Throughout this book, I have discussed bringing qualities I feel I have experienced during meditation practice, including calmness, insightfulness, empathy and general neutrality, into different life situations. As we have observed, being aware of the Five Hindrances can help one understand the 'ups and downs' associated with being diagnosed with Asperger's Syndrome better. But to be able to cope with different experiences, pleasant and unpleasant, including noticing and managing their impermanent nature, it helps one, through qualities of the cultivated mind, to recognise and balance what the Buddha described as the Five Spiritual Faculties:

1. trustful confidence and faith

2. mental strength, vigour and energy

3. mindfulness

4. concentration and mental unification

5. wisdom.

Trustful confidence and faith

This faculty, that I have gradually developed through bringing the neutrality and joy that I have experienced during Samatha practice into daily life, is a useful tool, I find, in terms of overcoming the hindrance of ill-will. It has helped me understand that holding onto my own thoughts and views, or distancing myself from the views and thoughts of others, can be creating the root of conflict, leading to ill-will. As well as different ways of thought, I have also understood through this faculty that ill-will can arise out of issues such as jealousy, envy and personal biases, which can be related to one's social conditioning.

To experience ill-will or friction between others, based around personal differences, can create a lot of stress for a person with Asperger's Syndrome, which can also expose one to the hindrance of restlessness and remorse. For me, I have found that this faculty enables me to be aware of the potential causes of ill-will so as to avoid it. However, if I experience ill-will unintentionally, which can be done much easier than one thinks, I have also realised through recognition of this faculty that the best way to respond isn't with one's own ill-will, as this leads to often false accusations of blame, which only creates enemies.

The neutrality that I have experienced during practice of loving-kindness (Mettā) meditation has enabled me, when feeling angry towards others, to concentrate anger, and to recognise acting on one's own anger outside meditation. This has helped to put behind me much agitation from past instances of bullying and ill-will that I have experienced as a person with Asperger's Syndrome, to the point where I understand other reasons for their actions towards me and do not lay blame.

Mental strength and energy

This faculty is a quality that meditation can enable outside practice in helping to overcome the hindrance of sloth and torpor, as the purpose of meditation is to cultivate the mind which helps one concentrate mind energy. As a person with Asperger's Syndrome, I feel I have begun to understand that my difficulties with flexible thought have arisen through not being able to recognise mind energy 'locked up'. During meditation, when focusing on the breath, a neutral object that neither excites nor depresses enables a neutral mind state that helps me notice areas of my mind that I didn't initially realise I had, such as the ability to understand and respect other people's views and opinions as well as understand difficulties others experience besides my own. I feel that this has opened me up to flexible thought, a quality that I am gradually being able to apply to situations where such ability is required, including in situations involving negotiation and debate.

Mental energy can also help one recognise mental strength, something else that I have often struggled to display when required, often resulting in me being easily led. For a person with Asperger's Syndrome, being easily led can lead the individual to unawareness of illegal activity. Mental strength can enable effective independent thought, and I have found that when in 'hopeless' situations, where negotiation is difficult, if one is able to show others that they are not weak, then at least a compromise can be reached.

Mindfulness

By far the most-discussed quality in this book, this faculty of the mind, I feel, can be of great benefit to a person with Asperger's Syndrome if able to recognise it. I have found that recognition and development of mindfulness through meditation has not only enabled me to recognise who I am, but also who I am in relation to my surroundings as well as being able to recognise the sources of different mental states, both negative and positive.

Through recognition of this faculty, I have begun to realise that much suffering I have experienced in my past relating to being diagnosed with Asperger's Syndrome has been the result of 'irrelevant' distractions, including at times comparing myself to or viewing how I measure up to others. Mindfulness has enabled me to realise that where suffering and frustration originate from is giving unnecessary attention to such irrelevant distractions, including wanting to emulate others.

How the quality of mindfulness is applied can be variable among individuals, often depending on their experiences. I have found through recognising mindfulness that it helps my self-esteem to review my progress and set goals in accordance with my own capabilities rather than others' expectations of me. Raising my own standards too high can lead to delusion and disappointment when realising I might not be able to meet them for various reasons. Mindfulness though enables me to be realistic in terms of aspirations, helping to overcome the hindrance of sense desire.

Concentration

Of qualities associated with Asperger's Syndrome, the faculty of concentration is often very visible in some individuals diagnosed with the condition. However, a difficulty that a person with Asperger's Syndrome may have is being able to balance it with the other faculties, to the extent that it clouds them out, attaching one to fixations.

Personally, I have found that it helps, as a person with Asperger's Syndrome, to balance this faculty with that of mindfulness, as this not only stops the person becoming lost in their own world, including within fixations associated with Asperger's Syndrome, but also helps to recognise and apply the faculty of concentration to overcome the hindrance of restlessness and remorse.

Effective concentration balanced with mindfulness, I find, helps me to avoid becoming attached to worrying thought, so that I am able to assess and manage different situations and mind states more effectively. Being able to apply this faculty to situations that require attentiveness, such as undertaking training or participating in a lecture, seminar or workshop, allows me to absorb material under study more effectively, as well as being able to apply what I have learned more mindfully.

Wisdom

Something that people I know with Asperger's Syndrome are very good at doing is accumulating vast amounts of knowledge. A problem though that many people with the condition, including myself, often have is being able to convert knowledge into 'wisdom'. Personally though, I believe that as a person becomes accustomed to and appreciates being diagnosed with the condition of Asperger's Syndrome and experiences the ups and downs associated with it, they can develop wisdom through learning from related experiences.

Like many people with Asperger's Syndrome, when wanting to achieve in life what one sets out to, I have found myself feeling like giving up, and in some cases have given up on what I have initially set out to achieve. When this has happened, I have often felt it has been due to me not being good or skilled enough to achieve, but more so because of a difficulty of being able to 'see' what I can possibly achieve. To do this requires concentration of mental energy to assess the situation accordingly.

Through learning from experience, and applying the other spiritual facilities, knowledge accumulated can be converted into wisdom.

Though it helps a person with Asperger's Syndrome to recognise the spiritual faculties discussed above, what can be difficult in relation to the way many Asperger minds work, is being able to balance them. As already discussed in this book, perhaps the key to being able to recognise and apply the faculties is being able to balance mindfulness with concentration. This enables a person with Asperger's Syndrome to retain their Asperger characteristics while developing further awareness of their immediate surroundings. Mindfulness can also aid in balancing the other faculties, in terms of watching out for any of the Five Hindrances.

CHAPTER 14

Epilogue

University reunion

One of the themes that this book has covered is being able to see people from one's past as they are now, including those that one has experienced friction and even conflict with . A concept in Buddhism that hasn't been covered in this book though is the notion of Karma. Karma, meaning 'action' in Pāli, is often applied to future results of past actions, including how false or malicious actions can result in suffering. As I have discussed much in this work, actions by or towards a person with Asperger's Syndrome, especially undiagnosed Asperger's Syndrome, that have negative effects can result from things being tried to the best of intentions but having reverse effects or simply through misunderstanding. In this case, Karma can help one atone for past actions.

To give an idea of how these themes can apply effectively to situations where one meets people from their past, I have taken my university reunion (from my undergraduate years) as an example. I felt as though I experienced friction with some people with whom I did my undergraduate degree. As little aware of it as I was at the time, one of my former university colleagues had been 'tracking down' the 'Class of '99' from Teeside University for the purpose of holding a reunion, to mark more than ten years passing from when we had first entered university together. I still occasionally see people with whom I did my Master's, but had not, until contacted, seen or heard anything from those who I did my undergraduate degree with.

The former colleague had found out about me and contacted me through my personal website. I got an initial surprise when I recognised the name of who one of my e-mails was from. Then when I opened it, I was more intrigued by the content – that someone I knew from my university days was planning a reunion. At first, I wasn't entirely sure whether or not to reply to the message, never mind attend a reunion possibly with some people from my past that I hadn't always had comfortable relations with. Through mindfulness that I had since gradually developed, I then began to think of the idea of seeing people from my past as they are now and, through seeing them this way, I could possibly repair difficult relations, rather than holding onto past instances.

Replying to the e-mail, I mentioned to my former colleague that I wasn't sure about whether to attend a reunion, due to the difficulties I had experienced with others from those years in the past. However, I was surprised at how positive the response was. She mentioned that other people from the Class of '99 had often asked if anyone knew anything of me, including what I had been up to since graduation in 1999 and even had 'fond memories' of me. But something that she then told me that I felt really invited me to be part of the reunion was that it would be an opportunity for former colleagues who felt guilty about the way they had perhaps been to me to meet the 'real me' rather than the guy that nobody understood.

Thinking of what one of my former primary school teachers had said of how he often felt frustrated with himself, more so than with me, wondering what to do to 'get through to me', this insight enabled me to realise that there was a similarity in this sense with my former undergraduate colleagues. As my colleagues with whom I did my undergraduate degree knew me as both a person with undiagnosed Asperger's Syndrome and diagnosed Asperger's Syndrome, they probably experienced similar confusion, and missed out on knowing who I really am.

Attending the reunion, I found it did me much good, meeting people who I had studied with, including both people that I had some difficulties with and those I remember being very supportive towards me after I returned to university after experiencing depression. Something I found from this experience was how people, not just myself, can change over time, as I found myself getting on so well with people who I had had differences of opinion with at university. One of them even admitted that she felt she was a 'nightmare' when a university student, but I was also able to admit that I had, at times, become 'cut off' through holding onto left-wing opinions.

Through this experience, I felt as though I was able to relive what I had largely missed out on when an undergraduate university student, as well as renewing past intimacies. But what was perhaps even nicer was how we were all happy for one another in regards to how our futures had turned out since university.

References

Attwood, T. (1997) *Asperger's Syndrome: A Guide for Parents and Professionals.* London: Jessica Kingsley Publishers.

Bhuridatta, Phra Ajaan Mun (2000) *The Ballad of Liberation from the Khandas.* Kuala Lumpur, Malaysia: Wisdom Audio Visual Exchange (WAVE).

Brahmavamso, Ajahn (2003) *A Dhamma Talk on Addictions and Obsessions.* Available at www.bswa.org/modules/mydownloads/viewcat.php?cid=4, accessed on 1 September 2008.

Dekker, M. (1998) *On Our Own Terms: Emerging Autistic Cultures.* Unpublished paper.

HH The Dalai Lama and Cutler, H.C. (1998) *The Art of Happiness: A Handbook for Living.* London: Coronet.

Mitchell, C. (2005) *Glass Half-Empty, Glass Half-Full: How Asperger's Syndrome has Changed My Life.* London: Lucky Duck.

Munindo, Ajahn (2006) *A Dhammapda for Contemplation.* Harnham, Northumberland: Aruna Publications. Available at www.ratanagiri.org.uk/Book/book5, accessed on 1 September 2008.

Munindo, Ajahn (2005) *Unexpected Freedom.* Harnham, Northumberland: Aruna Publications. Available at www.ratanagiri.org.uk/Book/book4, accessed on 1 September 2008.

Sumedho, Venerable Ajahn (2004) *Intuitive Awareness.* Hemel Hempstead: Amaravati Publications. Available at www.buddhanet.net/pdf_file/intuitive-awareness.pdf, accessed on 1 September 2008.

Williams, R. (2006) 'Interview: The Good Childhood Inquiry.' The Archbishop of Canterbury interviewed by James Naughtie, Today Programme, BBC Radio 4. Transcript available at www.archbishopofcanterbury.org/627, accessed on 1 September 2008.

Index